FOREVER NIGHT (Siempre Noche):
The Alternative New Year's Day Spoken Word / Performance Extravaganza
- 2017 Anthology

- First Edition.
- Volume IV in a series.
- 140 pages.
- Trade Paperback.
- American contemporary poetry anthology.

Contact Information / Order Online:
http://www.alternativenyd.org/

Rogue Scholars Press
http://www.roguescholars.com

Design and Layout: C. D. Johnson
Publishers: Rogue Scholars Press

ISBN-10: 0-9840982-4-0
ISBN-13: 978-0-9840982-4-8

Published by Rogue Scholars Press
New York, NY - USA

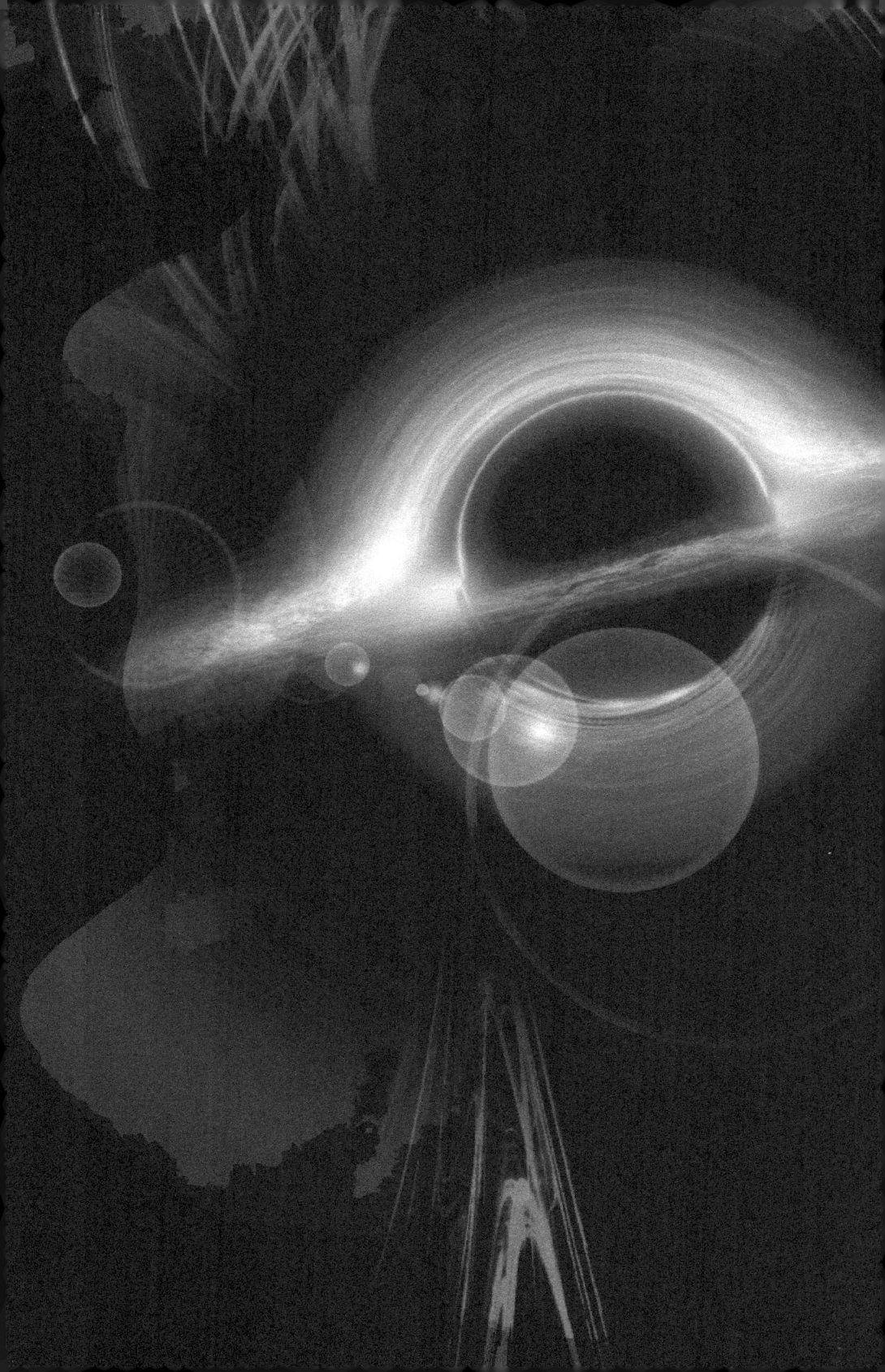

Forever NIGHT

Siempre Noche

**The Alternative
New Year's Day
Spoken Word / Performance
Extravaganza!**

2017 Anthology

http://alternativenyd.org

CONTENTS

CONTENTS Continued...

CONTENTS Continued...

APPENDIX

ACKNOWLEDGMENTS

I want to give a special shout out to our staff
for their help in making all this possible:

Madeline Artenburg
Pete Dolack
C. D. Johnson
Boni Joi
Ptr Kozlowski
Ellen Aug Lytle
Su Polo
Robert Roth
Thad Rutkowski
and Joanne Pagano Weber

I also want to thank the Nuyorican Poets Café
for welcoming us so warmly and generously
once more.

- Bruce Weber

Our 23rd Event And Our 4th Anthology... Amazing!

Every year I reconsider the broad strokes and possibilities, and the staff gathers in early winter to talk about new directions and bridges to cross. A major part of our planning is to reach out to new guest curators for assistance in keeping the channels open to new voices and sounds. We also hope to bring in artists we've missed, neglected, or not had back in a while. This year I am especially thrilled by the multitude of new performers that have been added to event.

When the *Alternative New Year's Day Spoken Word / Performance Extravaganza* began I fantasized about creating an anthology on the spot, with the help of an industrial strength photocopy machine nearby. Now in the age of the internet, and the publishing possibilities the internet has conjured up, plus the masterful hand and eye of C. D. Johnson, we have our fourth annual collection of a selection of works by participants in *Forever Night: Siempre Noche*.

The theme *Forever Night: Siempre Noche* was chosen in the course of this past overheated summer of Trump and Clinton, and after the theme was selected by the vote of the staff, some staff members wondered if it was perhaps too dark in its insinuations. Now, following the autumn election, we *must* and we *shall* persist even harder in our artistry, clinging to art's ever present truth to get us through the forthcoming night ahead.

- **Bruce Weber**

Austin Alexis

The Tale

Who am I to say
she was crazy?--
that woman from the neighborhood
I didn't know well enough
to predict she would say
what she howled from her stoop.
She told of an entity that appeared
at the foot of her bed.
Maybe he represented her dead husband.
Maybe he or it was an angel,
nearly invisible, but there,
seeable as mist and water are intangible
yet tangible.

Who am I to say
she was hallucinating?
In former times, people spoke of visitations,
demons, glowing spirits.
Perhaps in our modern era, we've lost
the ability to perceive these beings,
be they benign or wicked.
Except, once in a long while, one of us
like the lady from the neighborhood,
breaks through to their dimension,
then watches them with the wonder,
the awe of an ancient tribe
beholding a super moon.

———

Joel Allegretti

Cello

For Daniel Berrigan

Leviathan
Of the orchestral
Sea

Violin's
Magnification
Of itself

Cellar
Of the string section's
Architecture

*

In his closing decade
Pablo Casals
Played it

For world harmony
He bowed
It lowed:

Dona
Nobis
Pacem

His weapon
Of mass
Redemption

————

Amber

Mushroom

Don't call me a "shroom"
Don't drop bombs and compare the cloud to my shape
I can be beautifully fleshy, seductively colored or hidden as a fungus
My underground mycelium can cover the globe
One organism holding two thousand two acres together
My DNA and your DNA are fifty percent the same
I've been around for millions of years, give or take
a few thousand
And you have barely discovered my medicinal properties
Allow my secrets to awaken you
Do you see unusual light effects and enhanced coloration?
Are the mountains breathing and dancing as they ripple on the horizon?
Can you melt into the environment?
Do moving objects leave trails behind them?
When has music vibrated through you so profoundly…so deeply?
Has your temporal sense expanded to admit the
never-ending solstice?
A huge fungus called agarikon may be able to cure
small pox, TB and bird flu
Broom, flume, plume, consume, kaboom
When species die, we lose a part of ourselves.

———

Madeline Artenberg

Apostle

Bless me Mother for you are gone
and I still sin in the hallowed halls of cinema;
nay, I am wiped clean after each showing.
Like an apostle, I followed you, mother,
followed you, queen of the double feature,
followed you into forgetting
myself, you, hard edges.

You taught me to bless the moving image,
sweet and tart fruits doled out
in two-hour portions;
you taught me to slip into other skins
as easily as we slipped into disappearing.

There was no need for the talk between us—
the cinema sirens showed me their game:
Natalie, Doris, Elizabeth,
Marilyn, bad girls and good,
seduced by rock-hard jaws.

There was no need for your seesaw rules—
I learned the commandments from jewel thieves,
double agents, pregnant nuns;
rule number one—never get caught.

When the show was over,
we'd walk the two miles home,
pink slowly fading from your flushed face,
puffy mouth and eyes receding into rigid lines;
your love for cinema tucked back inside
that place I could never find.

When the show was over,
I returned to wanting
what you could not reach,
returned to waiting,
waiting to live,
to sin,
to be cleansed
in the hallowed cinema
of beginnings, middles, ends.

———

Ron Blum

Quiet

Why won't you let me be quiet?
Why do you get so irate?
What is wrong with being quiet?
Why this anti-quiet hate?

Why are you opposed to quiet?
Why do you think quiet's strange?
Why does quiet so disturb you?
Why must I adapt and change?

Why do you insist on noises?
Why are you obsessed with sound?
Why do you persist in talking
Every time that I'm around?

You don't like it when I'm quiet.
Why can't you just let me be?
There is nothing wrong with quiet.
There is nothing wrong with me.

Why do you insist I must be
Quiet 'cause I'm feeling blue?
Could it be, perhaps, or maybe
I don't want to talk to *you*?

———

Peter Bushyeager

Beautiful In The Glow Of A Spell

I'm attracted to people
I think I've met who look like
trending movie stars with
wide-spaced eyes
that I read as spiritual,
thick hair like a hat
that makes hats unworkable in
nude scenes nipples like
pebbles not cones or
discs because
that's what I grew up with.

They all turn out to be
pragmatists who slid into
chairs a long time ago and
won't be vacating the premises
any time soon.
You could consider them
wrecked in an ancient way like
old people discussing
old problems so old
they made their living on
the water with hand-tied nets.

I go to bed with
what I'm thinking:
celebrities launched to
thrill us in silk sheaths or denim
flicking toothpicks in their mouths
sometimes letting them
stick to their bottom lips
as they slouch in front of
green screens doing
a tough tease
with no off switch.

————

Patricia Carragon

The Divine Comedy

You wear many masks,
sit like a flag-waving jester—
throw tacos and spitballs
as we act out our lives.
We're your deplorable jokers,
alt-right Confederates,
gun-happy rapists,
Mother Earth wife-beaters.
We repeat our mistakes—
use different methods
to kill off each candidate.
As the wrecking ball
crosses the stage,
you and your punch line
can't find the exit.

———

Tina Chan

Rich Or Poor?

Rich Or Poor?
Are you rich with financial wealth
Or, rich in good character?
Are you poor stricken with extreme poverty welfare
Or, poor in malicious character?
Is one humble with good will
Is one filled with immense compassion and genuine concern
Inadequate with sincerity
Insufficient care
Narcissist addict
Selfish
Superficial
Disrespect and crass
Brash and impudent
Heavy acts of cunning

Rich Or Poor?
Focused value: quantity vs. quality
A man can bask in financial wealth, great height, good education, stable
profession
It all means nothing if a man cannot uphold honesty or hone good interpersonal
skills
A woman can glow with beauty, wrapped in designer brand name clothing,
adorned with expensive jewelry
It all means nothing if a woman cannot carry grace and humility with the
authenticity of her true colors beneath
Are you rich with good morals and a conscience?
How can such a person like you who's elevated be so poor in character?

Rich Or Poor?
In the thick of it
Be an instrument of change
The whole is greater than the sum of its parts
The emerging truth separated from falsehood
A radiant spirit with a good heart is the truest riches
How does one quantify folly and wickedness?

———

Lydia Cortes

One Day

I'll do it one day I'll get so tired and that day I swear I'll go away

*Uno de estos días me voy me desespero y me voy lejos muy lejos de aquí
sitio de solo Desesperanza me voy sola solita*

You kids drive me to *Desesperanza* despair all of you with all your things toys
clothes all over this place I can't pick up fast enough before there's a whole
mess again chaos in this place of

Too many things to take care of too much furniture to dust polish too many
clothes to wash to hang out the window then iron then put away in too many
drawers three closets and still your brother doesn't talk with all of this you
are driving me to despair you girls always laughing teasing your fighting your
brother with nothing

To say it's too much I'm supposed to take care of too much it's chaos so I sit
here so much time in this hard chair in this kitchen till I can't move just sit here
eating sliced white bread and butter can't take care of you two of your silent
brother can't take anymore his banging his back on the couch back and forth all
day except when he's

Here with me in the kitchen while I fry up slices of orange sweet potatoes frying
and frying for he eats mounds I fry while he eats just about all he eats is sweet
potatoes then he's right back to his couch so now its springs have burst broken
out torn straight through the velvet fabric sticking out like strange wire curls
sometimes

They look like skinny arms reaching out arms wanting even begging needing
makes me sad the rest of the body must be buried buried deep in the couch's
insides the couch where the boy he keeps banging banging his back back
and forth doesn't stop so that he's made a hole in the couch and a hole in the
wall behind his beloved couch you can see the plaster see the wood slats that
hold up the wall I can't hold on can't hold it up can't put it back together how it
belongs

The wall that should be still whole still *sano* in one piece but it's got a big hole like the one inside me that's almost funny if I could laugh can't there's too many things to take care of who's going to take care of me then it starts all over again the clothes getting dirty so many clothes you three your father get too dirty need they need washing need hanging starching ironing folding the floor needs sweeping mopping beds need to be made food must be bought must be cooked so I despair *me desespero me desespero y*

Me desespero hanging clothes on the line out the window I look down when I hang look down down from here it's so far to the ground from way up here on this fifth floor all those stairs need going up going so far so far down if I could I would I would just jump out the window and fly away fly so high God would have and keep me up in the air I'd go away fly far

Away somewhere where there's Peace everything neat everything clean and put away if I could fly I'd get away *adios so* far up so

High I might even meet mi *Señor Jesú Cristo* so together we would be in the place of Peace only Peace only all neat clean and put away

----

John Reid Currie

Hot Fall, Two Boys

Unexpected sun
against this window
glass and thick curtains

from the Protestant
church sale, safety pins
hold them up.

Outside, the trees that are green
a slow memory; summer heat
blanches them like family

photos of foreign places
fading in moldy sunrooms; our
innocent, plastic, exaggeration.

I never read about us in the newspaper
or the Wonder Book of Knowledge, the
sharp water, one hot fall in Queens.

I want to leave; become in India
one of the many, a devotee
of Ganesh, splashing water

in worship. Hit drums,
wade in the Arabian sea
all the hard small, waves

pushing against my legs,
fat boys in the bend
of the water;

points of danger
their edges cut
this many times.

———

Steve Dalachinsky

faces on the wall - reprise

(at the village vanguard)
- for neeli cherkowski

this is a wall i've sat in front of for many years
nter-mezzo
the structure of boredom / the boredom of structure
trading 4s with the air conditioner
in just the right place
& all those names reconfirming themselves
like old friends
faces of long dead melody makers i hear
inside my head
even when there's nothing there but exhaustion
bill, joe, sonny, dexter, trane, monk, jackie,
alone together
sitting this close without ever mentioning your name
of course i never saw you here but know
that secrets often kept bring dark recollections

something shines there all bent out of shape
a reflection of repressive freedoms
bugs in & out of lamplight

tomorrow may or may not bring that little used word
"PASSION"
stiff like a fetus floating
in a bottle of piss
but tonight the 3/4 moon & its beauty
come so cheap -
yet there's no one left to buy it.

—————

Terence Degnan

Churchville

because I was Eight
and told a man my secrets
you too, will have to live out these biopsies

because a guardrail once tried to halve
my Old Man's Olds like a cantaloupe
you will have a phantom nostalgia

because I snuck into a preacher's house
because I drank from the baptismal
because I cleaned my brother's scars
because I surfed a station wagon
because I smashed a bee with a Ouija board
because I saw the local drunk
wander naked through the tennis court

because the morgue is filled
with practice stiffs
you will give a pint or part
because I was born in Catholic skin
you will kiss a jaguar
because I was born with hidden ribs
sharpened after lockdown hours
you will give your love away
to kids without a lock-pick kit

because I bought time in Mexico
with a woman who gave the money back
you will live a life of debt
as burn marks pock a mattress
because I fed the hungry man
you will hunger for a litany
and suffer the foreclosure years
rife with evaporated testaments

because I named you after Azrael
or one of his kissing cousins
you will talk to men that haven't died
because your legs will blush in cloth
men will spin golden fish
from narrow vows and pocket rings
buy you powdered funnel cakes
give you things you throw away

because we were drunk for most of us
and drunkenness is why we rise
and punch a clock that butterflies
because I was named after mission bouts
after laborers mummified their fisticuffs
for the now and dying Irishmen
who decimated my Pop, the whether weight
before the pious and the flock
you'll be spared the rod a touch
you'll be snaked by modern plagues

because I was placed in the river bassinet
of family names that populate
before Christ struck down the Challenger
before the Second Vatican
you will be a monologue
to spare the world another mouth
you will be the ghost in the Trinity
the only part that's evident

————

Pete Dolack

Big Bang

If there wasn't a universe
It'd be boring
Nothing
Just nothing
If there wasn't a Big Bang
There wouldn't be anything to do
Just a point
Packed so tight you couldn't see
Nowhere to go
The other side of the point wouldn't be any different
Someday the Big Bang might come
That's what the physicists would say
And then it would be different
Until then you'd have to wait
If there wasn't a multiverse
There wouldn't even be a point
Waiting to explode
Or a universe
Or anything
Nothing
It would be so boring
No matter
No stars
No planets
No cities
Nothing

———————

Jim Feast

Trish,

Trish,
this sun above me
tai yern
swinging witlessly through the underbelly
of clouds

These stars
sing sing
like cat's eyes
peeping from behind rolls of a fat comforter

tin hong,
this sky, trish
into which I plunge my hands

this moon, yut lern,
only an eyelid left of it
I can't see your face there

But I see your face under there

every morning, trish,
every morning when the sun goes down

————

Bryan Cornel Fox

Untitled

Part I

I'm all bout love but bring fire and I'll bring fire. You think you know what hate is?
I got no patience
Good and evil what the fuck you make it
Get on that AA shit
and ask God to grant you the serenity to accept the fact you aging
No games I ain't playing
I'm all for the prophet but guarantee you'll see Satan
I'll send you to the depths of hell where I came from
right back to raging, total war be what I'm waging
The ink that bleed on this page when you turn the page and
see the kind of the rage that got you living like you trapped in a cage and eats your soul whole
This young generation hearts be stone cold
like December
that's that shit you going remember
So disarm all arms because before you know it you'll have a needle in your arm
It's what hate is, venereal disease contagious, come get a taste of it

Part II

I'm the devils tongue searing through south Bronx windows back in the seventies barren waste lands
the crack era, cuts in funding for education
at the hands of Reagan, 88' man, devastation
I reign terror like baby face kids that dump clips
on loose lips, sinking ships, torrential downpours
Hurricane tidal waves, when gats wave, white flags wave, when it rains it pours
This that flow that bring cats to they knees like a pipe do to a crack feign
gats scream, the smash team, it's in your best interest not to fuck with me
I'm doing my best to deal with this mediocre hand I been dealt
and Paxil, zoloft, and Thorazine don't help
The director of the psychiatric facility said "sorry son oh well"
He and anyone else that didn't give a shit including my mother could go to hell
I'm too strong
I've kept at it, an ex-drug addict that kicked habits and moved on
So let lames come at me to hell I will be sending them
and behold the pain I felt when I inject you with that venom

Daniela Gioseffi

Billions Of Gallons Of Blood

Think of all the pounding hearts,
lakes of tears and echoes of laughter:
more than seven billion
human lives throbbing.

Rhythms inside rocks,
atoms spinning in everything,
planets circling space,
man-made clocks ticking everywhere
in tidal rhythms, held by our moon.

Worlds turning in trillions of universes
expanding, traveling with their suns
and here on our small planet Earth
our rock home full of molten gasses, people
arguing, killing each other over their gods.

A grandmother combs the hair of a child.
Her hands move in a ballet of water
running over stones in rivers,
flowing like love to thirsty mouths.

Creosote beneath the earth protects
fence posts keeping them standing,
but, branches eventually break
as worms chew in the rhythms of clouds
floating across skies changing shapes
viewed like Rorschach tests to those
who rest on their backs looking up
into endless blue floating puffed white.

Secret are hidden in throats of caves,
screams of waterfalls, rustling leaves,
stirrings underneath, our dead reborn as grass.
All's wondrously, awfully here
each life among billions as one merges
into another, a mysterious hand
of creation picks up a book
between thumb and fingers and reads:

the time of galaxies, crustaceans, primates
since corporeal Earth began 4.5 billion years ago
and *Homo sapiens* arrived
merely 200 thousand years ago,
pumping billions of gallons of blood.

———————

Bob Heman

CODA

& they lived inside
of a little room
where the waves didn't come
& the wind didn't blow
& all around
at all the windows
little faces peered inside
& there were no voices
& no songs
& outside
behind the faces
something strange
was happening to the sky
& night came into the little room
& all the faces
let out a silent sigh
& it was over
all of it
& even the air itself
began to die

———————

David Huberman

Uninvited Visitor

It's a few weeks before 2017 and I already have an unwanted guest. A mouse…No not ATOMIC MOUSE, MIGHTY MOUSE OR MICKEY MOUSE! Just an inconvenient, germ carrying, grotesque, monstrosity. The creature had the nerve to show itself with all the lights on and run across the stacks of books that I collected to sell on the Amazon Web site as a third party seller. "Please God", I scream out. Don't let it's nest be in that section of my apartment. There goes the profit margin! Nobody is going to want to buy a book off the internet smelling of funky rodent. Demonic! Rabid! Putrid! Zipping through bags, shelves, and piles of paper collectibles, rare documents, out of print books. "MOUSE" I yell out, "don't die now!" From some poison that you might have picked up in someone else's residence that was ready to deal with fiends like yourself. The stink would never leave my packed studio apartment. Then even the Swedish/Russian blind woman in apt 7R wouldn't ever come over again. "Just leave vermin, take your diseased bacteria with you and never come back!"

———

Ngoma Osayemi Ifatunmise

Politrickery

Demockery
teeter totters
on the precipice of our discontent
put thru the microscope of integrity
coming up deficient of honesty
as the college elects to misrepresent
those crying out for proof
that the so-called constitution is constitutional
not just archaic babble
left over from centuries past
guarded by laughing gargoyles
on the steps of justice
apathy
is the aching tooth of dracula
fangs dripping middle eastern oil
as fat sam needs a colonic
500 years of lies
backed up in his constitution
constituents tired of being pregnant with hope
seek out abortions
feeling voting has no purpose in this hypocrisy
where the two headed coin
has two bad sides
and any way it falls
oppression rules
martial law hiding in the shadows
waiting for the eagle to fall
conspiracy theories ignored
while those who disorder the new world
wait for its deliverance
to the gates of hell

———

Kate Irving

Family Math

My grandfather was an alcoholic. His daughter,
my alcoholic mother, had three children.
Her third child lived only three days.

Number one, my half-brother,
whose father was alcoholic,
is a recovered alcoholic. His daughter,
my niece, whose mother is not alcoholic,
is also a recovered alcoholic and has
one child whose father is an alcoholic.
The child is seven, so far so good.

My father drinks but is not an alcoholic.
I'm number two, and I drink too,
but don't think I qualify as alcoholic,
a practice denoted as personality altering
to a destructive fault. My sons' father
lives by moderation in every way.

My younger son doesn't much care for drink,
my older son surely likes his and his wife
does too, conclusive of nothing to date,
though she is the child of an alcoholic.
Their two children have my love forever,
fingers crossed for that gene pool lottery.

———

Evie Ivy

The Walk

I want to drape my head
and become one with the night.
I look up at the moon—
a ball in the sky that seems
protected, wrapped in some
diaphanous tulle—yet

in its perfectly round phase up there.
The night is not moonless.
Tigers have stripes, zebras
have stripes, but you can't be
confused. Put a pig in a palace
and it will still "oink" at you.

What could change? And what
should? Maybe, only the moon?
I look up at the tulle moon.

In the darkened sky it looks safe
and snug in its transparent bag.
Elegant, it seems to complete

a picture of the sparkling night.
Tiger is tiger and a zebra
is a zebra. And there is nothing
to change. I pull my scarf
and drape my head and become
one with the beautiful night.

———

C. D. Johnson

Tara Devi And Some Crêpes

For a while, I was dating this militant atheist who used to sleep over every weekend. She was also a bit younger than me and «didn't know nothin' 'bout nothin'», as she put it. She was ex-Catholic, so she did know something about religion, but knew nothing about Hinduism.

Every morning I get up, I empty out my pant pockets and separate the coins. The quarters go into a container for my laundry money. The rest of the change goes into the bowl on the altar next to my murti (statue) of Tara Devi who is my ishta-devata (personal goddess of choice).

One morning, my militant atheist girlfriend asked me why I kept giving offerings to the statue? "Is it so the goddess will answer your prayers or something?" - she said in a snide tone. I said: "No, I don't pray. It's to remind me that I need to be a good and generous person today. There is nothing realistically making me be a good person, so I need to reinforce the behavior on my own. Otherwise, I may embrace indifference instead. That's why I do it every morning, in case I forget."

"So why do you take the quarters out?" - she asked, having had her curiosity piqued. I said because the money eventually goes to charity, but Tara who is a goddess of wisdom as well as wealth wouldn't approve of me giving away anything that was useful to me. And I need quarters for my laundry.

"Yeah, that makes no sense." - she said, but I am pretty sure she didn't think it did.

I didn't say anything else. I just went to get breakfast - her breakfast not mine since I never eat breakfast.

A few weeks later, we got into a fight on a Friday night. I remember it had something to do with which one of us acted the worst when we were drunk. She still slept over that night. The next morning when we were up, she asked me to get crêpes for breakfast. I screamed at her: "Get your own damn crêpes!"

She got up from bed, walked over to her purse and started going through it. I figured she was looking to see how much money she had for crêpes. She then pulled out some change and deposited it in Tara's bowl.

I asked her what she was doing? I thought she was going to say she needed to remind herself to be a good person. But she said: "You forgot to do it this morning. I didn't want you to forget."

I rose up from bed, got dressed, and went out and got her breakfast. She cooked dinner that night to reciprocate. It was awful, but I ate it anyway.

————

Icegayle Johnson

Begin

It's all to familiar- the fringe on her skirt
His hands touch lightly she moves the way she should
I watch enchanted wanting to know more

We all move in time to the music then laughter
takes over we smile in sync and come to a decision
we can't move forward the mood changes

What makes a life want to live again--
The miring sun, the night moon- desire- dreams-
nightmares-a voice says "I want to live" I really want too!

What can you say after you hear someone say
"I want to live" I really want too!
A lump in your throat, eyes weld up

It's all to familiar and to sad all at the
same time-that's a lot of fucked up shit-
to listen too and remember- yes-

Now, him, I remember (out of nowhere your memory flashes-
- I remember, how I wanted more then anything
to feel what it feels like to hold this fantasy

for years, the magic is the time line we shared
that in it's self makes this moment last for ever
someday sometime when you're all alone with this emotion

I'll be there too wanting to feel that rush that ecstasy
the incredible breathlessness, the smell of you-your mouth-
always in a memory-one memory that doesn't fade

———

Larry Jones

Megalomania

If only there were
a now for us,
a name for who
we are together.
If only there
had never been
another poem,
we might be free,
you and I of
my case history.
And if you would
acknowledge me
please keep it down;
that's if you're any
good in bed at all.
And if not please just
try to forget it.
There's no language
to remember
what was never
on my mind, and
no there are no
secrets in love and
yes the entire
world is listening.

Meg Kaizu

In Sand

Love is made of sand
That is why it spills
When I gather it in my hands

Like mother's flowing hair,
Cold skin,
Vacant stare into the distance

Lifeless clouds sing
Goldfish in the closet
Rain and snails on leaves

Sailors upon waves
Lost, forgotten
On foreign shore

I don't love you
I don't want you
Don't you get it?

Shrieks of ghosts in my room
Maze of my imagination
Daze of my dreams

Dead bodies upon
Dead bodies
Endless red horizon

We sometimes eat snakes
And drink water
Where our dead friends float

Sanity is made of sand
That is why it erodes
When tides rise

———

Linda Kleinbub

Carnage

They sit caddy corner
at the back of the bar
full of poetry and alcohol.

Romantics left empty
share stories, heartache and anguish.
Raw and honest,
with hearts exposed,
they take turns
slice slivers of heart,
place them on the bar.

Tales of a slow death, lasting too long
drama of a love that shattered spirits
mourning a companion lost in a bottle
memoir of a marriage held together with strings.

They reminisce all night
slicing slivers of heart
until the bar is red
covered with blood.

Carnage of lonely souls.
She looks into his blue eyes
which reveal behind sorrow, passion.

Words evaporate,
leaning in she whispers, "Kiss me."
Lost in each other
for a moment they are healed.

———

Ron Kolm

Round The World Cruise, 1934

(Composed from memorabilia found
in used books in the Strand Bookstore.)

She smiles at me
Then leans back
In her deck chair
As we end our vacation
With a cruise
Across the Pacific.

We'd found fun impossible
In trouble riddled
South America--
The hotels smelled of urine
The carpets were worn
And a gaucho broke her heart
With his bullet-studded belt.

We fled on a train
Packed with refugees
Sleeping car hotbox wheels
And the engine on fire!
We made it to Munich
And partied
The rest of the season.

A full Moon
Shines high above
The black waters
Of Repulse Bay--
I twist in my seat
And return her smile
Wondering how much money
We still have left
In the bank.

Tomorrow
We'll drink ourselves
Into gentle oblivion
But I'll try to remember
In the bottom of my brain
Not to let the guide
Trap us in his shop
Until we've seen
All the sights.

————

Ptr Kozlowski

Intercom

Please let me into the realm of your senses
Won't you grant me an audience
in the parlor of your touch.

Please let me in from the mindless exuberance,
the dizzying self-absorption,
and entitlement run amok.

Please let me into the fragrance of your breathing
I want to walk around in rooms
that are styled by your thoughts
And move in a circle of friends who all admire you.

Please let me in from the coldness of the logic,
from the Bad Eye,
and the wisdom of the Market's invisible claw.
Won't you grant me access to the
green zones of your whispers;
I wish you could give me a backstage pass
to the dressing rooms of your dreams.

Please let me in from this overcrowded city -
it's all filled up with humans,
and there's a lot of them I don't like.
Please let me into the realm of your senses
Won't you grant me an audience
in the parlor of your touch.
Why don't you be a dear friend now and come on,
buzz me up.

Art Lasky

A Zen Approach To City Driving

"Sonofabitch! Signal! If you're turning: signal! is that too much to ask for? Now I'm stuck behind you, ya bastard... What are you a spy? The CIA must be following you; is that it, you don't want them to know you're turning? ...It's clear, turn already! Can't you hear my horn? Jesus. Okay great...damn, red light...Good, the crossing signal is blinking, 5...4...3...2...Shit! an old lady with a walker, come on grandma move it, life's short, especially in your case. Oh great, sure, stop and rest mamala, no rush, you're holding up traffic, but don't worry, it's not like I have a life or anything.

Whew okay...great, gogogo! BRAKES! Shoot, I'm stuck behind a pick-up truck with North Carolina plates, can you drive any slower you friggin' farmer! Come on, yeah that's it nice and slow, don't you have to go home and plow the north 40?

"Gee golly would you look at all them tall buildings, maw would never believe it, I bet they got indoor plumbing and everything, shazam."

...Shit, now I'm stuck behind a damn woman driver, come on, come on, come on! Either drive or get back in the kitchen, why the hell'd they ever give you the right to vote? I should've had the dealer install a disintegrator ray; this damn horn is doing nothing!

Oh wonderful, a garbage truck...that's it guys, load one bag at a time don't strain yourselves. Yeah, and make sure you stop to chat and admire the scenery while you're at it. Friggin' city, friggin' garbage men. I don't even know why you're picking up in this neighborhood, you should be delivering. Come on, let's move it, pretend you're not a union guy, and actually have to work for a living. Okay...

Damnit, Jaywalkers... get outta the way ya bastids, what are you deaf? can't you hear my frikkin horn. I'm not gonna stop, that's it run you animals run! Next car I get'll have 50 caliber machine guns mounted on the hood. Oops, cop car, better slow down, I'm not gonna be part of this guys ticket quota. Let him find some other sucker.

Hell, red light... Okay it's green, hey you, in front of me! wake up it's green, d'ya think I'm honking for my health, a-hole, move it's the only shade of green they got, hit the gas you color blind moron, Go! Okay...

Damn bike lanes, jamming everything up…and the bikers don't use 'em, no they still pedal along getting in the way of traffic, bunch of friggin' degenerate retards, that's what they are…

Frig, now I'm gonna be late… Parking spot, come on, where's a damn parking spot. There! … Shit that Nazi in the Mercedes beat me to it. Frick, frick, frick on a stick; now I'll have to pay for parking. But at least I won't be late for that anger management class, I'm teaching.

————

Jane LeCroy

A Little Death

I carry a little death with me
on my back, in my bag:
cigarettes, my poems,
my attempts at impossible hopes,
a lighter, illegal herb in a one-hitter,
dirty secret photos, poems by others,
folded love letters soaked by rain.
What is man but his problems?
A lifetimeline of mistakes
knots on a rope a finite length
we end at a loose end, forever
undone but finished
we're left hanging by our dreams.
We never get enough of that sexy lover
or the bad-ass bass-line or the laughter
from our baby girl in the surf the first time.
If only the sweet sound could sing forever
and I could keep the whiskey high,
the buzz on my lips from the kisses I need
as a mother, a wife, a lover, a human hungry
for things to stay the same- when everything's good
but we're brought down again and again
we continue our relationship
with gravity until the grave,
we're saved when we think we're saved.

———

Linda Lerner

One Daylight Saving Hour

I am testing its limits
reaching back thru time zone years
to see how much can be crammed
into a single daylight hour, saved
in a space no bigger than
my first Manhattan apartment:
I take what I need, people give me
make what doesn't go together, fit;
look ma, no hands, I cry riding my first bike
riding words across a blue lined grade school notebook
so fast I couldn't stop, riding with my first man
on a creaking bed in hot Mexico City
out of breath in a future he didn't
belong in & someone else quietly
slipped out of in the middle of us:
it is an hour like the universe
continually expanding that I want to give
to another, show him how much
can be packed inside, never been
good with numbers I try to get him
to forget about logic, just feel
where my words are headed

———————

Phillip X Levine

Who Is Language?

Who is language that stumbles in with stutter and lisp yet pronounces all its p's? Who is language that chips thin blue ice from thick red air and tosses pitch after wild pitch? Who spins tales like tops and carries us to grandma's house or the darker sides of moons. Who unpetals the rose yet still leaves it smelling sweet whether naming or un-naming it. Paints castles in the air and invites us in for tea and smoke, then opens dungeon doors and says "go on, go down, go see".

Who is language and is he she and does it matter when change is just an or away? That gives and takes, this or that, then puts it in his hat and says "Hello, how are you? I am fine and are you hungry? Have some more of me. And drink and drink and drink some more, it's here, it's good, it's free." Gives fever pitch and measure and tosses earth and cloud together and then by magic brings a storm that rages in between.

Who is this that twists his tongue to shapes we've never seen? That burrows to our core of hearts then takes us to the stars and counts most every one. Who climbs atop the heads of pins and knows every angel's name, who takes time, adds lime and gives us rhyme. Who hands us rubies and tells us what they're worth and what they're not, who takes our masterpiece and hangs it on the wall face back and says there's more to do, to tell, to paint and tells us paint again.

Shall we call him friend, this churlish Merlin, this palmer of cards, this beast that creeps about our legs and licks our hearts, our arms, then singes the hair about our eyes and brings those eyes to burning? Who soothes our soul and scalds our tongue. Who bubbles blood, and crackles skin and then can also chill the bone to still, and freeze our lips as on a winter lamppost.

He is the stuff of knowing and the silence knowing brings. He is the sanest madness and is never mute, but babbles as the earth erupting, spilling red ore of mantle broken. So shall we follow him, he that bites us on the ass even as we hang on to tails? Who spits fire and perfectly round oranges and webs of delight and desire and then dissolves to thoughts, perhaps I might be dreaming, where chance is the stuff of certainty. Or exactly that reversed. Where might and what might be, is, and all that is, twists once like shifting blinds until maybe is not so. Like smile creeping or frown of glee, language boxes surprise like presents, bow and glitter and shiny promise, but inside only air. But something grows in the space of telling and that is green and live and breathes and that is us, or our knowing of us, and that's who language is or what he does.

Who is language? One may never know, but if it could be told, it doesn't matter, the telling is the story. So speak or chant or sing. Or whisper if you wish. Open up and out, and out aloud, the words are hers and his and yours and ours. And by so doing we become the gods around the fire.

————

Tsaurah Litzky

Full Lotus

Yoga has no margins, commas or apostrophes,
sometimes it's full speed, sometimes all subtlety,
it keeps me guessing how far I can go,
it shows me what I reap, I can sow,
Yoga is a billow, a pillow, a plow to break sorrows,
Yoga means working hard and letting go.
I sit spine erect, legs spread in front of me in a V;
bending my right knee, I bring the right foot in, place it high
on the opposite thigh, then I lift the left leg over the right,
put the left foot high on top of the opposite thigh,
it took me four years to get this right,
my Aunt Mildred who introduced me to Yoga once said,
"You will never do Yoga, your legs are too fat,"
but here I am, now in Full Lotus, breathing, breathing deep,
as I float up, up through the swelling streams of consciousness,
up, up, through the roaring rivers of time
to the rich, briny oceans of open mind.

———

Ana López-Betancourt

reflections

he showed up
when the core
of a massive star imploded
funny
he was like a black hole
a mysterious light swallower
hiding all his intentions
like a furtive cosmic criminal
his intense desire
for annihilation
camouflaged his aching need
to sever the bonds
between past and present
and yet the split
left him yearning
for connections
i saw it all - but i denied it...
time passed - and i allowed it...
then we became vicious...
while he thrived
in clandestine matters
i became sinfully forthright...
behaving like matter
and anti-matter
we collided
to annihilate each other...

––––––––

Ellen 'Windy' Aug Lytle

leaf / november, 2016

a leaf floats between
two birches

the field is shocked;
its lofty manner
its deliberate
slowness

maybe it's jealous of the dance

she watches the moment
go by as if it's on fire

such haste
such ferocity

he watches her
watch the moment
then grabs his own

together they might
stall the twilight

————

Stan Marcus

Chrome Yellow

You, painter, wearing your rag knuckles
in the yellow downpour as you slap thickly
at the bistro and hear who knows what
on the cobblestone alley and the street leading
north and south. You know you are empty,
and the pallid walls that are perfect in their tones
of gray and make up the rooms where you sleep
and you eat are rendered imperfectly yellow and useless
and hold up nothing at all. What is it you feel
when the fishmonger pushing his cart is suddenly
set up behind you and leaning his eyes on
your shoulder and you are unwashed and unfed and sniff
in those miserable walls the blisters, the veins, the friends,
the yellow inside of you pouring all over the street?
It is summer and winter and the sky is so dense
you can bang a nail into it and hang up your coat.
You settle yourself on the red blanket. The green
shutters that are behind and in front of you open
and close, but you are unaware of the seasons
for time measures nothing for you.
You decorate with your flowers, and the cane
chairs that have slipped into corners and wait
patiently for whoever will have them are yellow,
and so are the pillows and the sheet, but the walls are a thin
blue because you and your pigment are dwindling.
There is an ear and a candle, and the train chugging
over the trestle is an element and not a way
out. But you are not looking for ways out.
You are planted in a yellow puddle and the effusion
of colors is drowning and feeding you, but you
have no intention of budging because you are
incapable of doing ordinary things. The house
must be assembled and filled, and it is you only who know
the inside and the outside and it is for you to tell me
about it and it is for me to listen because
I know you are suffering and that under the cobalt
sky, to the north of the streetlamp and above
the brothel, you are slowly dying of yellow.

———————

Peter Marra

Room 26: A Deadly Organ And Controversial Toys

noir collapse
caffeine. no food.
pit of stomach is blinding. hollow finish.
approaching notes thrown out at the sea
swallow love. chew.
chew it up.
shards of distant memory.
faded family photographs
swallow. chew. thrown at the
water
a function of mate selection
via early spread eagle positions
in fashion
in the center
committed during life
afterlife destinations.
it's really hard to hold still
a blindfold for good conduct
that satisfies the clients in any order
the 13th assured him it would be empty
the blouse came off
no resistance
into one or more chambers of wanting
with each pass,
no resistance.
her spot was synonymous with treason
as she finished with a digital camera
she convulsed up
just to relax, and not squirm around
imbibed a purely humanitarian drink
"give me your limbo," she said
in a voice that quavered
then she turned off her name
"i wondered why you were talking.
you read me pretty well..."
she put on a pair of naughty
appendages that craved their former owners
who were hidden in the closet.

"eat your libido.
you know what?
i want to know how
priests think.
start the sex playlist,"
she said to no one in particular
a linear story. divine history.
she slid one finger along undetected.
the ability to view those fabulous lips pulled apart
displaying kaleidoscopes in a warm, dark hole.
her eyes were glazed slightly, and continued to evolve
into deeper shades of black
greased animal slippery
emerging from dwelling underground or
from living in trees with the defrocked priests and nuns

_____

Jesús Papoleto Meléndez

Affirmation Of Myself

When I am forced, by the complicated circumstances of human nature, to ponder the definition of my life and the possibility of its purpose; that there may in fact of science be a purpose bestowed upon this Spirit of myself as I walk embodied in this human form; to form a life of meaning from the sand of time before me – I am forced to this inevitable conclusion:

That I am indeed a poet, and as such compelled to experience the totality of the experience of my feelings; to attempt in earnest the understanding of their complexity, apart and yet united with all other forms which, too, experience their own complexity;

That I am made in a design to question everything that happens; and to attempt to be so acutely aware of every moment that passes into life as I observe it; and yet not falter in the shadow of my experience of pain; to continually seek and find the joy and miracle routinely in the daily twirl of life; to discover the extraordinary in the seemingly simple and mundane, and to report it to the peoples of the world;

That I, whomever I am – whatever is my name in the soul of the Universe – must continue to feel life, and expose my sensibility like skin to the vulnerability of feelings, needing only to understand that Poetry is about Empathy – Empathy for all in life; to exercise the odd ability to place oneself in someone else's shoes in life, and to stroll their walk in the sympathy of imagination; and that, therefore, I must be brave and strong with an intangible weakness;

So that in the cosmic order of incomprehensible reality, I may come to understand that not everyone understands everything...
That it takes the make-up of everyone in order to make up the contemporary world; And all the intelligence within it is contained in the memory of the living as inherited from the deceased; That the present is composed of the past; and the future is but the androgynous child of their union. And that if, indeed there is a God, It has designed me so, and therefore knows my soul much more profoundly than I or you are capable to understand; thus, I have nothing to explain of myself to you, except to comment on the observations that I make myself.

———

Nancy Mercado

Catcalls To My Brain

No 1980's tight young ass to pounce on anymore
No smooth skin to assault anymore
No frightened little girl to follow
Down cold shitty Lower East Side streets anymore

Now-a-days the boys catcall my intellect
Corner me in conference rooms
Universities
In restaurants

¡¿Oye mami cuántos libros has leído?!
¡No sabes na bruta!
¡¿Where did you graduate from mami?!
¡Your university degree means nada nena!

They attempt to inflict
Injuries with blank pages
To drown me out
Under piles of exclusions
To erase my existence
To whittle me down
To a stub

N o t h i n g

Silence.

These days my catcallers
Are the intelligentsia
Postmodern jeering elitists
Hyperbolic hipsters swooping in to take charge
Our modern-day land grabbers
The white settlers of the information age
Revolutionary revisionists
My cat-calling boys come with females in tow these days
Sold out dames of trendiness
Fast talking fools
Puking memorized conceptual hullabaloos
Living delusions

They are lost souls

Existing in their own holograms of fame
Convinced masses in the world
Know their name
Believe their immortality

Don't my catcallers understand
They have yet to be born?

———

Dennis Moritz

thank you

red wine works takes the edge off thank you bacchus
tensions in the news what's new about that where's my red hat

i am swimming now in the standing water lake huge and smooth
microbes are farting methane and co2 at the outlet of the hydro dam

love the sparks love the slope of stone no it's concrete if it was a
pyramid monumental and inert

i love the lies so constant are they insects or birds what living things
love us so i love the piping sound i am so empty at times hear it

that's a lie there i love my lies any fiction any hard work of imagination
what's the diff does it change us change anything are we living in bodies

is the world green then brown then exploded yes everything moves
inconceivably fast away from a core i know it's an image only a conceit

when i love you does everything reassemble o those trees love them
the painter who does the landscape i love the painter who does the paint

———

David Moscovich

Undercover Island

Maria tell Mitchell about her eldest cousin, an eighty-eight year old virgin who live on the island, in a place where there were always very few men — a deeply religious woman who never married and who lived with her brother until he died.

When the family go to visit her they are astounded by the many statue of saints she keep all throughout the long hallways of a richly mirrored house. Is not because they are placed on nearly every surface — a collection of Mother Marys above the stone hearth, another Mary nestled between seventeenth century candlesticks, St. Guadeloupe on the lion's paw roundtable by the ancient blackwood settee in the entrance, St. Fatima and three more Marys surfing the doilies atop the hand-carved oaken hutch.

Is not how she would tour everyone through, rosary in hand, proudly displaying the saints, and there were dozens of saints — but she would be sure to mention that after her brother passed, she discovered these very handy coverings he left in a bedroom drawer, small but expandable, and built with a convenient, easy to grip rounded hat, not unlike a bejeweled mitre, to cover the head of the saint, and an extensive flexible portion which could be unfurled to overlay its body. She just knew that he had intended to armor the saints with them, and that he died before he had a chance to.

In his honor, she cushion all the saints with this miracle plastic. Nobody in the family or anyone else in the community have the guts to tell her that these are made from latex, and that the coverings are called condoms, which are used in the act of sexual intercourse and not as a dust-barrier for the holiest of Catholic saints. This has gone on for years, and she continue to display her saints, shielded with prophylactics, to everyone who visit her on the island.

_____

K B Nemcosky

Double Down

not the tabloid rumor I started

how he slammed Harrisburg

if he doesn't win on the majestic

banks of the Susquehanna River

how he slammed Gold Star family

Khizr & Ghazala Khan

how he slammed Colorado firefighters

for saving him from stalled elevator

how by tiny pink fingernails

he tossed out baby at Virginia rally

"You can get the baby out of here"

how all babies are immigrants

come crying into this New World

reaching out for god knows what

babbling a first language

————

Valery Oisteanu

Hedda Sterne

Hedwiga, Heddi, Hedda
Quiet sister of the Bucharest avant-garde
Fleeing Romanian antisemitism
Escaping through forbidden roads and borders
Of war-torn Nazi-Europe, shouting in German
Cold winds and giant waves of the Atlantic
Don't bother her while" The Little Prince" is born
Protected by the strong shoulders of Antoine de Saint-Exupery
Loving, and sketching, poets and artists
So many strong women friends like Peggy, Betty, and Anne
Fritz, the savior, and sheltering husband
Saul, the sarcastic tormentor
As the quiet wife of a depressed genius
Struggled to keep him alive and creative
A sole female beauty among Irascible men
Featured in LIFE magazine
Riding a Packard to Vermont
To paint the phantasmagoric farm machines
Driving a Cadillac to the Springs, Hamptons
The car concealing a ghost that resembled Igor Stravinsky
Over the bridges and highways of surreal America
The art history of the 20th century stacked
In your studio, every ism, a flux in flux
Art and life reflected in geometrical paintings
Of Alaskan landscapes, circular intersecting roads
All recorded with her eye camera
The sphinx never smiles, just paints
Her end arrived slowly at the centennial mark
In the blind darkness, in the concrete jungle
At the intersection of 71st and 3rd avenue
The soul flies via exit 13 on FDR toward the East river

Jennifer-Leigh Oprihory

Note To Self

after Jon Sands
You haven't earned the right to break. Get yourself together.
Note to the man who broke me: Get the fuck out of my poems.
Note to my poems as of late: You smell too much like sunrise
to be a rude awakening.
Note to awakenings: You look better on Virginia Woolf.
Note to Virginia Woolf: Scientists have officially proven the existence of death
by heartbreak.
You never needed the water.
Dear water: I sometimes worry that we are an Oedipus complex
just waiting to happen.
Dear Oedipus: If 3's the charm, then why do you die at the end of the trilogy?
Dear Trilogy: 9's my lucky number. Try that on for size.
Dear Size: Stop making molehills out of mountains.
Dear mountains: I've concluded that you are only good for 3 things:
hillbillies, hiking, and horror movies.
Dear horror movies: The only reason we keep watching is
that we know the villain is partially composed of our own
skeletons.
Dear skeletons: Stop being so damn breakable.
Dear breakable: You are no longer allowed to be an adjective for anything not
made of porcelain.
Dear porcelain: Stop cracking on white people.
Dear white people: Stop teaching your sons that they are God's gift to mankind.
Dear mankind: Stop telling white people that not becoming a serial killer is some
kind of accomplishment.
Dear Casey Anthony:
Dear Reader: You totally thought I was breaking with form there, didn't you?
Dear form: You are sexier with the lights on.
Dear light: Come home. I'm not as afraid of the dark as I am of losing
my own shadow.
Dear home: Pick a favorite place. Now, STAY THERE.
Dear favorite: If you are reading this, it means I've dropped my walls.
Dear walls: It's going to be lonely without you.
Dear You: I'm sorry this took so long, but I've finally finished writing the book.
It's called "detachment" and it's written around all of the best parts of you.
If you can't make out the lines, use lemon juice.
Nothing that was ever worth it didn't burn.

―――――

Yuko Otomo

our yearnings to decorate things & ourselves (alike)

Whether boredom or a certain sense of general uneasiness is the fundamental background reason for it or not, either way, some bottomless, shapeless unnamable dark matter torments us. A fear toward *Eternity* urges us to possess things that indicate a clear identity of *Life*'s weights in our hands. Urged, we decorate ourselves. With flower petals; crowns; necklaces; names; medals; titles; abstract patterns; fame & etc. Like a loaf of bread with plenty of butter on it, we decorate ourselves with images of other (thing)s.

Spring, summer, fall & winter. According to the changes of light within the four seasons, *Boredom* & *Anxiety* make a seasonal noise. In order to avert our points of view from darkness within us, we invent things. In order to escape from the fear of *Eternity*, we put clothes on things & give them names. Praising things, comfortably swollen with the decorations we put on, we negate our own nights. Adding every imaginable shape & motif to our *Time/Space* that shares the same dark color with *Eternity,* we unnecessarily make it dustier than it deserves. Doing so, we indulge ourselves in our own, bright, yet warped, invented dreams.

————

Eve Packer

thanksgiving

high 93:
'ATTACK ON OFFICERS JOLTS A NATION ON EDGE'
after 9/11
you think thats it, &
after trayvon martin you think
no more, & after sandy hook,
you certainly think things
will change, then tamir rice, freddie gray,
eric garner, orlando,
and last week alton
sterling & philando castile......but then of course
5 police officers in dallas, and oh yes
the bastille day truck-kill thru
of 84 in nice, & yesterday a.m.,
3 officers in baton rouge,
that was july, today, 11/24 thanksgiving day,
gasping in red ketchup
map, fish on hook, glutted, gutted,
ready to choke, snap
and what can you say:
stop stop isotopes stop
but it seems it will get worse,
worser and worse, and no
brilliant image or words
for this how did we get here
and how do we get out
monster shape-shifter
universe--you under-
stand the ostrich,
and the gardener, the gardener
sprinkling
the plants, looking,
not at the too blue sky, the
fiery earth, not the growing
green, but the way water
glances off light

nyc.7.18.16: 2:51pm / 11.24.16: 10:57pm

Mireya Perez-Bustillo

Cumbia En La Plaza Bolivar

The drums sound across the vast Plaza
the Catedral on one side
the Palacio de Justicia on the other
in the center
the swirl of ruffled skirts
the piercing flautas de millo
I twirl my hands high
my back straight
my feet shuffle
to that cumbia beat
"Colombia tierra querida"
today peace sweeps del Caribe al Pacifico
de los Andes al Amazonas
the blood stopped
Today "Colombia tierra hermosa"
you move the drums, the rivers, mountains, llanos
You - me
en una cumbia de paz
cumbia de paz.

_____

Puma Perl

Waiting

Obediently,
I wait for permission to surrender.

Compulsion, as dense as the air.
Another year rolls past my wandering lips.
I promise you, I promise that I won't leave
this time, but I lie, I always lie, I lie down
on mirrors and memory, chance lost
like fillies on a running track, and I remember,
I remember my hands, no longer my hands,
I remember my legs climbing mountains,
I remember blood red arms and empty
sockets, today is tomorrow and I've grown
tired of my skin, tired of Renoir on the brown
couch, no barking dogs, no footsteps, no
whispers caught on camera; I pledge my submission
to the ground, you may keep your burnt skies
and scorched questions, my ears are burning
as we move closer to resolution, I promise
you again, and again I lie, I lie on shards of glass
and broken book jackets, and I remember
the way you touched me in parked cars,
and I remember your hands were mine,
and I remember your eyes falling
like apples, and I wait for permission
to surrender.

Obediently,

I wait.

———

A. Podracky

Walt's Florida

Soft winds from faded palm trees. Battlefield of the North far away. The body electric still sings at a turquoise terra-cotta square, the center of a community of Moorish styled homes. A bright green cart serves watered-down martinis and purple margaritas at the two o'clock afternoon happy hour. Knees repaired, hips replaced, new set of teeth, Walt joins a line dance to *Mustang Sally*. The other dancers mostly wide hipped women wearing tight hibiscus patterned pants and belts with red flashing lights. Walt ponders-can anything be done for the withered heart.

A silver haired man on a lemon painted bench watches Walt dance with the women. He puts his hands
in his Bermuda short pockets and finds his ex-wife's pearl earring. As he rolls the pearl slowly between his fingers he remembers her voice whispering, "Honey, put this in your pocket, I lost the other earring." Her false sweetness, so much sweeter in recollection.

The man shows Walt the earring when Walt sits down on the bench. "My wife's, from the islands, number three of three," he says with a toothless grin. Walt nods back at him, thinks, what islands? Later, on a ride in a pink golf cart covered with twin heart decals, license plate *Debbie*, the man grabs Walt and kisses him hard.

———

Ron Price

After Loss, The Going On

She sleeps near an open window
in a bed not her own,
lines carved around her eyes, her mouth.

Perhaps she dreams of pine trees
with small green cones
clustered on a branch,
or purple oleander, yellow broom.

Perhaps she hears the thunder
and boom of surf breaking the shore,
and long beaked birds
wing through her sleep in search of
what will feed their ongoing flight.

Perhaps, or perhaps not.

Either way, I know now –
lines carved around her eyes, her mouth –
there are among us wretches the lost
who will never be found,

and this scrap of a poem is for one:
a woman disappearing from the inside out,
as if memory were no more than vapor
risen from the grass

as easily as she rises from bed
without any clear thought

of what she lives for, who she loves, or why.

———

J D Rage

Andy Warhol

I
I've been bored with myself
since Andy Warhol died
spending my time
contemplating a nail embedded
in the pavement by the thousands
of cars
thousands of trucks
and bikes and motorcycles
and buses, you can't forget buses
they ride over the nail
it is a regular nail about three inches long
and 1/4 inch wide
ride over the nail as I watch
as if it were nothing
but if it is nothing
why is it shaped like a lightning bolt?
II
You've got to pay attention
to the streets
I once walked over a little metal star
lying on the sidewalk
it was shining up at me
telling me something
and life went on
but now I will never know
how my life would've turned out
how much it might have changed
the outcome if I had picked it up
III
I have dreamed about the silver star
and now I will dream of the nail
and I will dream of Pop Art
but dreams will never change
the fact that I have been really bored
with everything
since Andy Warhol died

_____

Jill Rapaport

The Rack And Ruin Of "Robust"

When you are born strong and healthy, with a loud cry, but you are scared and nervous and you don't trust others to leave you in peace while you sleep, you may find that you arrive, after a decade or so of life, at a stage of development in which the appearance of strength and robustness, while comforting in its pledge of self defense, comes to seem, perhaps because it is all you have besides your thoughts, unseemly. Yes, it comes to seem unseemly. You've been reading about elevated rangs of humans from the time you were old enough to read, looking at pictures of them with their standards on their horses, with their wimpoles in their windows.

The men, of which you are not one, are on the horses, while the wimpoles, of which you have none, belong to the women. You have tried to get on a horse and come down, and your one attempt at wimpole wearing was a sad comedy. You have watched the men ride out away on to open roads while you standing, or crawling, with your baby toys, gaped in front of the house and you have always refused to look back up at the nurturing wimpole in the window. There is nothing for you at either spot.

For some of these reasons and circuitously, at thirteen and with Jane, you began to see, observing Jane, that to be robust and hale/healthy, to be redolent of and radiant with strength, was not the path to a proper femalehood. You looked at the pale and small, the wispy and fragile, and saw in their stylized weakness, a possible way to go ahead. Weakness the genre you hated and always will hate – most of all when it comes upon you – but the distilled version, of the wearer of wimpole as swept up by the armored arms of the rider of horse, showed promise. You rode with it on to the open road of seventeen, eighteen, nineteen, and twenty.

It was the meeting of men and making friends with them that brought you, strangely, out of the wimpole world and into the world of the hearty and hale, and further, the healthy, the strong, and the commanding. You could have an effect on others. You had enough to waste and you wasted a lot of it. "A natural leader," someone said; "intimidating" said someone else.

"Robust," the word, was having its own evolution and rise to adulthood. You had blinked and looked again and "robust" the word had changed in meaning. Had had its meaning changed, maybe. They were using it now in some sentences like "There's a robust market for exchange-traded funds" and "Employment is showing robust growth." There was a wince that gave way to a loud, a robust cry; "robust" the word, like several comparable natural and innate glories, had been taken for alteration. How now, brave cow, could you reinstate it in your scabbard?

———

Robert Roth

Untitled

I've wanted to write a short story for many years about a young woman who dreams of being a famous poet, to be part of a culture of artists and poets, part of a world transforming community. She comes to New York from her home in Halifax. Through the sheer force of her belief that that community exists she approaches various well known poets, artists and musicians without fear or ego. She penetrates their cynicism, their despair, their competitiveness, the wall they have set around themselves and touches that part of them that is still similar to her. They become transformed.

She rises quickly in their circles. Things fall almost effortlessly in place for her. She is totally without guile. Her confidence soars, her contagious humanity reaching out to audiences throughout the city. She writes a book. She gives a reading at Cooper Union. And here I'm lifting a story Meyer Liben told me about Delmore Schwartz. The place is jammed. The first two rows are filled with homeless people. After the reading someone asks her to repeat one of her poems. Then someone asks her to repeat another. And so it goes until the security guards clear the hall. The curiosity and the excitement of the homeless gives her a sense that she has reached the masses. They of course just wanted shelter from the cold and the longer the reading, the later they would have to go out into the night. At some point it all starts crashing around her. I'm not sure how the story will end.

————

Thaddeus Rutkowski

Bad Monkey

The monkey was friendly. He was small, and she could hold him up to her face, where he would touch her hair and cheeks with his hands. He was a smart animal and liked to imitate humans. One time, he saw people lighting matches, so he decided to light matches himself. He held the book of matches in one hand, pinched off a stick with the other, and struck the head against the sandpaper strip. When the match flared up, the monkey didn't light a candle or the stove, or even a cigarette. He just decided to burn the house down. Well, maybe he didn't "decide" to do that, but he didn't know what else to do. He tossed the match, which landed on some curtains, and the whole place went up in flames. Or that's what would have happened if his owner hadn't snatched the matches from his hand and cuffed him across the head, not because she didn't love him, but because she wanted to save her home from destruction.

Sarah Sarai

Love Letter

The EpiPens I gave you.
The medical marijuana you
smuggled from New Jersey.
The time you rushed in
with a job lead on your phone.
I got the damn job.
It was twenty percent creative.
Which they'd promised.
Which made you excited for me.
Excited? I thought you loved me.
Planks are laid over my volcano.
No splinters, not a one.
You had me rub the Greek stone
before I walked over.
The old ways working, working well.
I would have climbed into you.
Every woman has her limits?
Like I don't know that.
Like that doesn't tear me apart.

———

Ilka Scobie

What We Lost

100,000 New Yorkers gone
Three plus decades of devastation
We acted up to fight a plague
Buried some of our very best

Hibiscus Harris/Ronnie Burk/Timothy Gallagher
Leslie Cifarelli/David Wornajovic/Sybil Walker
Artists, actors, poets, beauties
A lost constellation

How did a sexual revolution
turn to a blood born curse?
Ignorance begat isolation

Did our enormous loss
prepare us for 9/11?
We learned to mourn the unseen,
The unwritten, the young
The painful presence
of premature absence

We are left with voluptuous memories
If silence equals death,
Survival requires a hard core heart

Survival requires a hard core heart.

————

Hugh Seidman

Crossing Bryant Park

Susan Robertson (1943-1997)

Rink down—up last fall mirroring summer.
1200 steps to work—Seventh to Madison.

First, past 50—your bridal two-step.
New, wet grass invoking *tomb*.

.

Father: suicide; Mother: survivor; Sister: fatal breast.
Tai chi fighter, shrink, scholarship Bryn Mawr waif.

Lungs sicker than said or known.
Phone small talk—then you were gone.

.

10,000 years ago: not statue, urn, stone.
10,000 years ago: sexual proof of lives.

Left you that August—who shall say why?
Hammocked dozer; oil-slick lake rainbow.

.

10,000 years ago: hope—oldest karma.
10,000 years ago: friends— *forever*.

Also—noduled, cut out womb.
Transfusion, perhaps, the future tumor root.

.

Tall, rawboned girl, in a brown poncho.
Memoir of the body—10,000 years ago.
Tears upon tears—more than for anyone.
Susan—do you yet smile at dull woe?

.

High-heeled graduates' pale lilies, arterial roses.
A couple's extravagant, tortuous kisses.

Heard your name, as if called.
Neurons that will not be annulled.

.

Nothing to do but abhor the wind.
Implored the immortals for solace.

Smut-mouthed Brigitte: vulva peppers, black rooster.
Red-tongued Kali: lei of heads, corpse trampler.

.

Reached at last—furnace blast.
A few pounds of dust, ash, bone.

Carbon tundra turning under suns.
Born to your planet—less than a grass pebble.

———————

Brian Sheffield

[and suddenly // it all makes sense now]

and suddenly,
it all makes sense now—
the smell and
the taste of the atmosphere—
it's like smog
and steel, glass and
car exhaust, hot concrete, hot plastic, the hot
soles of hot shoes; its
smoke that falls out
from the street like
reverse gravity; a handle bar
mustache and
jean overalls, a gas tank
relieving itself on
the sidewalk. its an orange
sky that spills its
color over me; a torn
canvas; a dead
pigeon; metal grates where a
subway screams, its
a shadow that spreads its
fingers across the
wide expanse of the
americas; a loud boom resounding through the
red and brown
brick of a rent controlled apartment
complex; its an absurd comedy, a large and abstract
image chasing its own
tail; it smells like american
movie stars and
pungent colognes; car horns
blaring aimlessly at nothing at all—an endless drag
for talking suits;
dead dreams; hungry children
we are all
ignoring; gun metal, gentrification as
defined by
people who don't understand
gentrification;
and suddenly, it all makes sense now.

———

Susan Sherman

The Death Of A Thousand Cuts

No one blow alone is lethal
The poison builds slowly
healing seductive promising release
only to be opened at another time
in another place

Ling Chi The death of a thousand cuts
torture reserved for the vilest of deeds
or for the rebel The one who doesn't fit
The ultimate warning
where not to entrust the heart

Ling Chi In modern parlance
creeping normality
unacceptable propositions
occurring in small unnoticeable increments
until damage is irrevocable
Ice melting into water
filling the vastness of an ocean
dissolving from below

The obscene myth of vanquishing grief
Denial anger forgiveness acceptance
As islands are swallowed up
populations displaced

Live somewhere else
Leave what you love
Move on

As if love were a subway stop
As if you were holding up a restless queue
when what is dear to you is sliced away
first a finger then an arm a leg the heart

Ling Chi The scar remains
a network of twisted veins
How long before the point of no return
is reached

―――――

John L. Silver

In Early November

in early November
when i saw shadows moving back
before they turned to lengthen
in a different direction
in a different clinging
to a new path,
standing there
at the turn
in the clear embrace
of a broken life
i found you there
inside a brief moment
but perhaps not brief enough
to defeat reason

the drab eternal colors
and the temporary ones
surrounding us
with a mirror of sights
including a precipice
cutting through hands
grasping pointed cliffs
suggesting a surrender
to the air of birds
or gravity
letting go of this view
of reaching out
and autumn walking blindly

———

Miriam Stanley

Subway

Sometimes I want to grab a man,
Pull down his trousers on the train,
Whip out the part I need from his boxers,
Blink out fellow commuters like I'm Samantha the Witch
Or from Hogwarts Academy
Because it is ruthless dating online.
Last guy was a libertine posing as a turtledove,
We slept together until I said, "I love you."
The generations play a practical joke -
You're married with kids, or a spinster
Waiting for a hook-up.
Birth control wields its double-edged sword:
Women the magic act sliced in two;
Writing heals the split.
Some call that productive.
The world spirals: a harlot letting down her hair.
Penelope got back her man;
How long will the rest of us wait?

———————

Terese Svoboda

The Glass Of Champagne

I broke my glass and shards flew
       into the salad or
               my imagination
sliced off
the bad parts.

          In your living room,
we sat under blankets. We chatted
       and froze like penniless
    immigrants.   Thus swathed,

we argued over who loved us the least.

         Drink helped squire in
the newest year, a narration with both our
      foreheads creased,
husbands just
        a phone away.

New Year's stands there, clock hands
             wringing,
and bells.
         A cruel word hovers,
an insect twitches, weather-less.

The youngest should live
              longest
and know the least: the first
     lean years, the bad
breakdown - except for the reverb
     of tragedy,
the genes
     effervescent,
carrying it all anyway,
        bubble to the brain.

———

Lawrence Swan

Waiting For X

I am waiting for X.
The waning supermoon hangs on the sky,
a crumbling white disk in the daylight,
a pretty day in an invisible war,
in the Eye of an invisible storm.
It is early in the morning and I am waiting for X

I perform a mass for X, and contemplate X,
and wait for X to speak from the whirlwind

X marks Here or There in my unreliable maps.
Here You Are and There is where your treasure is.
Your treasure is buried in the abyss.
Your treasure is buried in emptiness.

X holds the fire of creator destroyer
X beats the drum of existence
X says Fear Not, I am unarmed
X indicates the revolutionary situation
X crushes the ideology of power and possession
X blows the horn that blasts down the walls
X dances in the temple
X takes a Giant Step into the unlimited

I am watching for X, and I am waiting for X within me.
X stands at the Door.

Alice B. Talkless

Faith

I have to accept dogma if I want to live forever
in the spirit world, to kiss ancient feet or rings
and the asses of many emperors, like Constantine.
He is the guy between me and Jesus, before I die.
He made room for all popular prophecy in his lifetime.
He was not amused by Metatron or any mystery
he could sink his fangs into and shake to pieces
then gulp down in short order only to vomit back
with a pledge to dedicate a holy day unto.
For fear of sins held against me after I breathe my last,
I have to make room for philosophical fuckery
in my tolerance belly, smeared with the slime of shame
looping through cosmic boredom, and no more time
for future resurrections or even one last prayer;
one last moonshot from the passenger window of a car.
I have to bend down, embrace a silly male,
pull up my skirt whether I'm on my period or not,
and get on with denying my eternally fouled intelligence.

————

J M Theisen de González

The Case Of The Grateful Granddaughter

I can't walk past a thrift or used book store without checking for Perry Mason novels. My affection for these is through my dad's mother. Divorce imploded my family; we rarely saw each other. Once, I asked Granny,"What do you like to read?" "Erle Stanley Gardner"was her reply. I was clueless at the time, but lived across the street from a great used book emporium, so crossed Brighton Beach Avenue to investigate

Twenty-five cent copies of weathered Mason novels were there; a quick read that I was completely charmed by, and instantly hooked. There is a certain comfort in writers that work with a formula. Each book is "The Case Of...": a finite period in the life of Perry Mason, counselor at law. Next, those fabulous covers. Pocket Book Editions of 1940s are especially lush. Sultry lingerie-clad women, with nipple-less breasts, and guys with guns. Open the cover for a tantalizing description of the crime story at hand. The foreword reiterates the author/attorney's interest in crime and justice, and elects an unsung element of the justice arena to single out for a dedication. The regulars are listed, with the page numbers where they first turn up in the case; either setting up the case, as in Mason: "His interest in the case began with a phone call from a frightened woman." Or Della Street's "Mason's Gal Friday--and all the other days of the week". The typical characters are Mason; his "confidential secretary", Della Street; Lieutenant Tragg of Homicide, Mason's nemesis/assistant D.A. Hamilton Burger; and Paul Drake of the Drake Detective Agency, a "partner in crime" (solving).

Perry Mason novels are a riotously politically incorrect read. A woman under the age of 25 is a "girl", as in "before him stood a beautiful girl, with light golden hair, and a glittering gun in her hand" from the jacket of "The Case of the Empty Tin". Mason and Street date, under the guise of business meals. Street's asides pass as some sort of freeze-dried flirtation to the passive-aggressive romance of these two. In "The One-Eyed Witness", Della Street notes that Mason is "a bachelor with a perfect right to take out your secretary to a nightclub".

That's not to say Della Street is a cream puff! Della's quick mind often saves Perry Mason's ass, by noticing nuances in expression and voice that Mason is too pre-occupied to catch. Such vigilance is met with an endearment. ("Darling!" is common) and a kiss. The case's solution is celebrated by dinner and an "evening out".

Part of the romance of buying things second-hand is that you don't know their origin. So, I wonder if maybe, by some fluke I might have gotten a book that could have once been Granny's. My Granny's final days were in a home; days and nights passed in a blur of dark and light; her loved ones--strangers she'd certainly never met. I prefer to imagine Granny much younger, curled up in her green chair, with a cup of milky coffee, and her Siamese on the ottoman; her bright blue eyes scanning the text as she tries to outwit Perry Mason. "The Case of the Grateful Granddaughter" is simple. Thanks to Granny for so many things; including many delightful hours of reading!

———

Jack Thomas

The (Secret) History Of That (Infamous) Magazine (Wall) Revealed!

Introduction/Preface/Epilogue/Afterword. This could be (either) the beginning, *or* (this could be) the end.

While others have stopped (doing it) retired (that dreaded word I swore I'd remove from my vocabulary. I have seen them come & go, fall off the cliff (deep end) by the way(-)side. Recently, someone I know on the West Coast (a photographer) said she had retired. I asked her: From what? She said: Life! I said: I know what you mean! If anything, I have picked(-)up steam!) not quit, moved on due to life (in general) death, old age, marriage, children, the job, etc., I have *not* (for some reason). I continue to do so (persist). Why (me)? Why *not* (me) might be a better question? What is it that keeps me going? Am I (fucking) crazy? Am I stupid?! (I don't think so.) What is wrong with me? I ask myself these questions all the time! I grapple with these thoughts. Wrestle with this notion. (Unfortunately) I do *not* have an answer. I write from some inner compulsion that keeps me going (pushes me forward) eggs me on (as someone I know once said (you)). I can *not* see (do *not* know) where it (this) is going exactly (taking me). I plan to keep on doing it as long as I can (have breath) ideas (until I run out of them). I do *not* know how much longer? At present, I see *no* end in sight! I am best known for how long I've been doing it, &, who I know. Rather than who I am, &, what I know (have done) my (own (personal)) accomplishments (of which there are a few). I am *not* (exactly) pleased (happy) with this (whole) idea (concept). This disturbs me to no end. Horrifies me. I would prefer that it would be the other way around. I see it as a lifetime thing (hopefully). I look (up) to others for inspiration. My idols are people in their 80s and 90s. As a child, I used to play a game, where I compared people's ages. The older they were, the better! I hope to be like them (one day) live as long as they have (done) & keep on (still) doing it (if I am (still) alive) live long enough (am lucky (enough)). From them, I get guidance & sustenance. Did I (ever) think I would (still) be doing it (over (30(-) years later))? *No* way, Jose! Never in my wildest dreams (fantasies)! At mid(-)career (another word I never much cared for (either)) here's to another 30 (if I live (that) long (enough))! We'll see? I hope so! ...

———

Zev Torres

Arrogance In The First Degree

It would be
Arrogance in the first degree
To assume that
You have anything
Worthwhile to say
Anything that anyone would
Find interesting enjoyable compelling
Anything worth retelling repeating
To assume that anything of
Intrigue fascination or sizzle
Ever happened to you.

Worse yet
The highest of crimes
A capital offense
Would be to insist that in fact
You survived a calamity
A crash a burn
A seismic shift
A collapse
A high-speed collision
A chilling encounter
An explosion an implosion
Unwanted unanticipated terrifying
Catastrophic traumatic
That ground your beliefs into rubble
Reduced your convictions
Into sediment --
And that you must speak of it
Must tell your story.

Yet that is the foundation of my faith
My original and perpetual sin.

––––––––

Anoek Van Praag

Obscene Beauty

Under the Tuscan Sun
Sotto il sole della Toscane
different from other suns
diverso da altri soli
I landed in my favorite town
on a hill sticking out
boasting its beauty
vanta la sua belezza
the cobblestones uphill, crooked
good enough to sprain your ankle
leading into another street with cobblestones
the past is under me around
in plants and flowers
their smells mixed with the ages
wooden doors that lead to lives
the girl gets slapped around the room
the sounds of silent cries
grida silenziose
the breeze outside just perfect
through small barred windows
muffeled roars from getting raped
we do not speak or hear or see
The water fountain from the wall
makes perfect trickles on the road
local Italian completes the story
Italiano locale complete la storia
the air is cool against the heat
the walls a yellow sand and rock
blood stained from wars we all forgot
Who built that archway in the end
leading to other lives
amidst the purple flowers
osceni cosi bella
obscene
so.........beautiful

———————

Claire Van Winkle

Next To A Man

What I loved best: the length
of him. I loved lying next
to a man so tall
I could almost feel like the child I was.
My favorite part of each night: not him
over or inside me
but next to me—
my hand on his hip,
my palm taking the sharp
turn past his sex to my love
at its height:
the moment he opened to my unskilled touch. His thighs
were delicate, such smooth skin and soft down—I loved
that when I lay beside him in the dark,
one of us felt like a woman.

————

Phyllis Wat

Tabulation

the word process of complicated ardor and time-based dynamic growth
systems create feedback loops unfinished out of principle as accordions pleat
into big cities with sensitive distribution centers of ugly beautiful colossal
bridges uncertainly sturdy and scaled like fishes or other eukaryotes from
humans to flowers to amoebae and closely associated archaea in our
incompleteness actively reworked and reintegrated into random objects such
that the alpine architectures of Angkor, Frühlichkeit and Air Colony are lifting
and playing with murk until death collects their memoria the way flying above
it makes it a cloud or riding in it makes it a boat as an early photographic
machine would engineer image so little to go on so crazy but so to the good a
propensity for the unconditional where the absolute finds ominous expressions
in rigid dystopias exploding to space warped with gestures of never no nope
but ragpickers collectives' infinite fragments morph to proboscis of complicated
ardor and time-based dynamic growth which create feedback loops' unfinished
sprawling of

————————

Bruce Weber

German Toothpaste

They called it German toothpaste
Cause when you were in the trenches
You couldn't exactly pop a bottle of champagne.
They'd lace their brushes with the stuff
And it would heal all odors.
Some of the krauts would laugh
When they heard the name
And nod their heads in wicked agreement.
Wars were different then before the bomb.
You could see the blood in your enemy's eyes
And things had a more intimate and devastating ring.
When Uncle Elmo came back from the big one
He would shake like an old jalopy
Simply from waking up in the morning
And seeing the sun rise.
I wouldn't want to put a damper on anything
But the more I think about it
The more I want to cry.
The salt cleansed my mouth
But my sores kept aching
And even God's letters to my wife didn't help.
I wandered the streets of my hometown
Like a ghost of some other age
When steel was King
And you could get a swig of mother's milk
For less than a dollar at the corner of Main and Vine.
I'd open my mouth and brush up and around
Till the salt did it's cleansing trick
And I'd pour my morning cup of java
And duck whenever a kaboom went by.
I'll never forget coming home
And squeezing that white pasty stuff
And living the life of Reilly
With my feet up and a smile for the democracy of the fittest.
My mouth clean as any victory in the war to end all wars.

Francine Witte

Selfie At The End Of The World

Like everything else, the apocalypse
will be photographed. Duckface crumble

of skyscrapers, or the twisty scowl of the ground
giving way. Sudden, but not surprising.

You'll remember the temperature rising
and the earth pulling off its sweater

of foliage and ice. How it all seemed
so distant, but now shows up to photobomb

that last TV reporter, humanity trampling
itself in the background. No selfie stick

long enough to fit seven billion,
so instead, you gather a bouquet

of faces around you, strike a pose and shoot.

———

Jeffrey Cyphers Wright

Boutonniére

for Miguel Algarin

The gods of Vodka River declare,
Death shall have no sway here,
my little problem child. My boutonniére.
At the Ding Dong Lounge on 105th.

Raised up on 6th Street and FDR Drive,
you're always down for cooked peaches
in Newport or San Juan. You regret
that "Men can't say 'chicks' anymore."

Dirty looks—I too know them well.
You must be a mold. "In the rear,"
you quip. Our bar stools spin.
Lit candles prick night's womb.

Let's go for a ride together on the Whip,
onyx-spectrum panther driven.

————

Anton Yakovlev

Dance Of The Sugar Plum Fairy

There was always a hint of that classic *Nutcracker* number
in my saunter down Tchaikovsky Street
from my job as a taste-tester at the candy factory Red October
to my second job at the candy factory Bolshevik.
I kept waiting for you to notice that hint.

When you received that genuine Wedgwood bowl
from all those Olympic teams you had led to gold,
did you think of my ballet school diploma,
or my triumphant reports on deluxe dark chocolate bars?

You see, you were never floored by the color
of my hair, you were never floored by the way
I checked my dress in the mirror. You were never floored
by my day-to-day choreography,
by the abandon with which I pounced on the lower octaves
of your candelabraed upright piano.

I knew we would miss our 50-year anniversary.
And I know we won't live to see our 75th.

Still, on that Leningrad white night,
hanging out with your track-and-field team, you tried
to hold on to the chestnut scarf I had dropped,
and though I snatched it from you,
I knew we'd end up together.

Now, after your third stroke,
I could dangle all the scarves I have ever owned
in front of you, and you wouldn't know they were mine.

I could ask you questions to make you figure it out,
make you Sherlock your way to the only reasonable conclusion,
but still it wouldn't click,
just like the description
of a chocolate bar's shape and taste
doesn't make someone blind from birth
understand the color brown.

Sometimes I rush to change your bed sheets,
go down to the laundromat,
come back to hug you,
comb your beard.

Sometimes I go to the store.
You smile: "Don't go!"
I fear those words will be the last I hear,
so I always hurry back home
down Lenin Avenue
with a loaf of bread.

––––––––––

APPENDIX

CONTRIBUTOR BIOGRAPHIES

Austin Alexis //

Austin Alexis: author of *Privacy Issues*, two chaplets by **Poets Wear Prada** and work in *Rabbit Ears: TV Poems*, *Poets4Paris*, *The Journal*, *The Pedestal Magazine*.

Joel Allegretti //

Joel Allegretti is the author of five collections of poetry. His second collection, *Father Silicon* (The Poet's Press, 2006), was selected by The Kansas City Star as one of 100 Noteworthy Books of 2006. He is the editor of *Rabbit Ears: TV Poems* (NYQ Books, 2015), the first anthology of poetry about the mass medium.

Amber //

The cornucopia fruit and vegetable lady, from apple to zucchini. Poems published, performed, taped, translated. Hosted monthly office poetry events. Amber illuminates.

Madeline Artenberg //

Madeline Artenberg's poetry has appeared in many print and online publications, such as *Vernacular and Rattle*. She won Lyric Recovery and Poetry Forum prizes and was semi-finalist in the 2005 contest of *Margie, The American Journal of Poetry*. Her work often touches on Jewish and New York City themes. *The Old In-and-Out,* a play based on her poetry and that of Karen Hildebrand, directed by Kat Georges, garnered raves in June, 2013.

Ron Blum //

Ron Blum is a writer. He lives in Boston, Massachusetts.

Peter Bushyeager //

Peter Bushyeager's poetry collections include *Citadel Luncheonette* and *In the Green Oval*. Recent poems in *Live Mag!* and *From Somewhere to Nowhere*, the forthcoming Unbearables anthology. Reviews and articles in *Talisman*, *Rain Taxi*, *The World in Time and Space* anthology, *Encyclopedia of American Poetry / Twentieth Century*, and Wave Book's forthcoming collection of interviews from the Poetry Project Newsletter.

Patricia Carragon //

Patricia Carragon has two forthcoming books: *Cupcake Chronicles* (Poets Wear Prada) and *Innocence* (Finishing Line Press). She hosts the Brooklyn-based Brownstone Poets and is the editor-in-chief of its annual anthology. She is one of the Executive Editors for *Home Planet News Online*.

Tina Chan //

Tina Chan is a lively poet whose writing style is a poetic puzzle. She believes words extracted from the heart are to be made memorable.

Lydia Cortes //

Lydia Cortes is the author of two collections of poetry: *Lust for Lust* and *Whose Place*. She has also been published in various anthologies and in online zines. Recently her work has appeared in the literary journal, *Upstreet*. Currently she is working on a memoir in verse form. She's very pleased to be included again herein.

John Reid Currie //

John Reid Currie was the founding editor of the journal, *Ozone Park* and writer in residence at the **Louis Armstrong Archives** and museum. His chapbook, *Others* was published by Ghostbird Press in 2015. **www.ghostbirdpress.org**. His poetry is featured in *Greenwich Village* published by St. Martins Griffin. Mr. Currie is a member of the writer's collective, **Oh, Bernice!**

Steve Dalachinsky //

Poet/collagist Steve Dalachinsky was born in Brooklyn after the last big war. His poem "Particle Fever" was nominated for a 2015 Pushcart Prize. His most recent books include *Fool's Gold* (2014 feral press), *a superintendent's eyes* (revised and expanded 2013/14 - unbearable/autonomedia) and *flying home*, a collaboration with German visual artist Sig Bang Schmidt (Paris Lit Up Press 2015) and *The Invisible Ray* (Overpass Press 2016) with artwork by Shalom Neuman.

Terence Degnan //

Terence Degnan is a poet. His most recent book, *Still Something Rattles*, was published by Sock Monkey Press in September, 2016. Terence produces the storytelling series, HOW TO BUILD A FIRE, and the poetry series, **Poets Settlement**. Terence lives in Brooklyn with his wife and daughter.

Pete Dolack //

Pete Dolack is an activist, essayist, poet and photographer who tries to keep juggling all these balls but, alas, keeps dropping some of them. Pete's book *It's Not Over: Learning From the Socialist Experiment*, is available from Zero Books, and his essays are published in his **Systemic Disorder** blog, as well as in publications including *CounterPunch*, *Z Magazine* and the *Ecologist*.

Jim Feast //

Jim Feast's poetry book, published in 2016, is titled *Time Extends Life to Those Who Survive*.

Bryan Fox //

Bryan Cornel Fox is a New York poet who loves to box and has performed poetry around the city at places such as Nuyorican Poets' Café, GLBT Center, Word at 4F, and the Bowery Poetry Club.

Daniela Gioseffi **//**

Daniela Gioseffi won an **American Book Award**, two **NYSCA** grants and **The John Ciardi Award for Lifetime Achievement in Poetry**. Her first of sixteen books: *Eggs In The Lake*. Her latest: *Blood Autumn*. Portraying her work in civil, women's rights, and climate justice, a docu-drama: **www. AuthorAndActivist.com** screens throughout the country. She edits: **www.Eco-Poetry.org**: climate crisis literature, appearing widely. Info: **Gioseffi.com**.

Bob Heman **//**

Bob Heman has edited *CLWN WR* (formerly *Clown War*) since 1972. His words have been published on every continent except Antarctica.

David Huberman **//**

David Huberman is the Ranter and Raver of NYC. He now has been put on the endangered species list!

Ngoma Osayemi Ifatunmise **//**

Ngoma is a performance poet, multi-instrumentalist, singer / songwriter and paradigm shifter, who for over 40 years has used culture as a tool to raise socio-political and spiritual consciousness through work that encourages critical thought. Ngoma weaves poetry and song that raises contradictions and searches for a solution to a just and peaceful world.

Kate Irving //

Kate Irving's poems have appeared in, among others, **BigCityLit.com**, *qaartsiluni*, and *Press 1*. Her chapbook, *Raising the Arsonist's Daughter from the Dead* was published by Finishing Line Press. She grew up in NYC and is grateful for that unique education.

Evie Ivy //

Evie Ivy has 3 books out, *The First Woman Who Danced*, poems based on her experiences as a dancer and dance instructor, *Living in 12-Tone . . . and other poetic forms*, *No, Nonets . . . the Book of Nonets* (Ra Rays Press). Some of her work can be seen online in several poetry webzines, including *Levure Litteraire*, *Versewrights*. She is host to the **Green Pavilion Poetry Event**.

C. D. Johnson //

C. D. (Seedy) Johnson: Former web developer, webmaster, and I.T. Director for CEO Clubs International, Inc. Currently, a freelance web, software, graphic design, and digital publishing consultant. Holds an M.A. in analytic philosophy and logic theory and a B.S. in computer science. Has taught adult literacy classes, introduction to logic, religious instruction in Sanatana Dharma and Shaktism, as well as Advaita Vedanta philosophy. Current projects include three books on philosophy, research into Indian Nyaya logic, and a book on conlang (constructed language) theory. He's the editor-in-chief and publisher of the *ANYDSWPE* Annual Anthology series (Rogue Scholars Press).

Icegayle Johnson //
_____

Icegayle Johnson is a pushcart nominee *"True Blood"* Rabbit Ears TV *Poems Anthology*, 2015. *"the key"*, 2012. Forth coming *Eclectic,* full length, summer of 2017.

Larry Jones //
_____

Larry Jones was the co-producer along with Bruce Weber of the first five **ANYDSWPE** events at Café Nico, his loft apartment / performance venue one flight above the Pyramid Club on Avenue A. An Associate of the **Academy of American Poets**, his work has appeared in many literary magazines and anthologies. He teaches literature and creative writing to gifted and talented youth at Hofstra University.

Meg Kaizu //
_____

Meg Kaizu has lived in Tokyo, Moscow, and NYC, contributing articles for magazines such as *Tokyo Art Beat*, *PingMag*, *Whitehot Magazine*, *Being A Broad*, *Metropolis*, and *New York Art Beat*. Her paintings, prose and poetry have appeared in *KD-Magazine*, *Avenue*, *Off-Yellow*, and *Otter Magazine*. She studied art at the University of Oregon and the Art Students League of New York.

Linda Kleinbub //
_____

Linda Kleinbub is a volunteer at **Girls Write Now**. Her work has appeared in *The New York Observer*, *The Brooklyn Rail*, *Yahoo! Beauty*, *Grabbing the Apple: An Anthology of New York Woman Poets*, *First Literary Review East*, *The Nassau County Poet Laureate Society Anthology* 2016 and *The Best American Poetry Blog*. She is also painter and organic gardener.

Ron Kolm *//*

Ron Kolm is a member of the **Unbearables** and a contributing editor of *Sensitive Skin* magazine. He is the author of *Divine Comedy, Suburban Ambush, Duke & Jill, Night Shift* and the novel *Neo Phobe*, with Jim Feast. Ron's papers were purchased by the New York University library, where they ve been catalogued in the Fales Library.

Ptr Kozlowski *//*

Ptr Kozlowski once worked as a deliveryman. He's been a cab driver, too. This poem was previously published in *PPA Literary Review*, Vol. 20. North Bellmore, New York; Performance Poets Association, 2016

Art Latsky *//*

Art Latsky is a retired computer programmer. After forty years of writing in COBOL and Assembler he decided to try writing in English; it's much harder than it looks. He lives in New York City with his wife/muse and regularly visiting grandkids. Art's had stories published in *Drunken Boat, Danse Macabre, The Cohaba River Literary Review, Third Flat Iron* and **Decasp.com**

Jane LeCroy *//*

Jane LeCroy: (**Sister Spit**, **Vitapup**, **Nu Voices**, **Ohmslice**, **Transmitting**) fronts the avant-pop-post-punk band, **The Icebergs**, with Tom Abbs and David Rogers-Berry. Three Rooms Press published her multimedia book of lyrical poems, *Signature Play*.

Linda Lerner //

Yes, the Ducks Were Real, was published by NYQ Books (Feb. 2015) as was my previous collection, *Takes Guts and Years Sometimes.* A chapbook of poems inspired by nursery rhymes, illustrated by Donna Kerness, *Ding Dong the Bell Pussy in the Well* was published by Lummox Press, Feb. 2014. I've been nominated three times for a Pushcart Prize.

Phillip X Levine //

Phillip X Levine lives near Woostock, NY and is approximately an actor, poet, poetry editor for *Chronogram* magazine and president of the Woodstock Poetry Society.

Tsaurah Litzky //

Tsaurah Litzky is a widely published poet, and writer of fiction, memoir, creative nonfiction, plays and commentary. Her poetry collections are *Baby On The Water* (Long Shot Press) and *Cleaning The Duck* (Bowery Books). Her sixteenth poetry chapbook, *Full Lotus* (NightBallet Press) is now in it's third printing. Tsaurah is working on a new poetry collection, titled *We Shake It*.

Ana Lopez Betancourt //

Ana Lopez Betancourt is a bilingual poet, theater worker and educator. Born in Loiza, PR, graduate of Boricua College, she has presented at **BACA Downtown**, **The Ear Inn**, **El Museo Del Barrio**, Boricua College, Rutgers University, Ramapo College, Hostos Community College, and **The Nuyorican Poet's Café.** Her work has been published in *And Then*, *Tripartita*, *Compass*, and *Breaking Ground*. The poem "reflections" was previously published by Robert Roth in VOLUME 7 of AND THEN 1996.

Ellen 'Windy' Aug Lytle //

Ellen Aug Lytle, or Elle, as she likes being called, is working on another poetry mss. which may pass the test with her publisher for 2018! she wants to definitely write a 'travel with myself' novella or series of short stories and, do more to help animals everywhere. Lytle loves to read and binge watch special TV series! She is a wife, mom, grandmom and sister.

Stan Marcus //

Stan Marcus' poems have appeared in *The Virginia Quarterly Review*, *Stand* (Leeds, U.K.), *The Literary Review*, *Prairie Schooner*, *College English*, *Poetry East*, *The Journal of New Jersey Poets*, *North Dakota Quarterly*, *Denver Quarterly*, *The Minnesota Review*, *Permafrost*, *North Dakota Quarterly*, *Grasslimb*, the anthology *For a Living: The Poetry of Work* (University of Illinois Press), and other publications.

Peter Marra //

Peter Marra's writings explore pain, addiction, love and obsessions. He has had over 200 poems published either in print or online in over 25 journals. His published works include *"approximate lovers (downtown materialaktion)"* and an e-chapbook, *"peep-o-rama"*. A new poetry collection, *Vanished Faces (a performance of occult infections)* will be published in 2017 by **Writing Knights Press**.

Jesús Papoleto Meléndez //

Jesús Papoleto Meléndez's play, *The Junkies Stole The Clock* (1974), was the first Latino play produced by the **New York Shakespeare Festival/Public Theatre's Nuyorican Playwright's Unit**. One of the original founders of the Nuyorican Poets Movement, Meléndez's political, intellectual and linguistic approaches in his work remains relevant. *Hey Yo/Yo Soy 40 Years of Nuyorican Street Poetry* (2Leaf Press, 2012).

Nancy Mercado //

Nancy Mercado is the editor of the *Nuyorican Women Writers Anthology* published in *Voices e/Magazine*, the Center for Puerto Rican Studies, Hunter College–CUNY; an online literary journal. She is a guest curator for the Museum of American Poetics and assistant editor for **Eco-poetry. org**; a web site dedicated to addressing the issue of climate crises. For more information: **www.nancy mercado.com**.

Dennis Moritz //

Dennis Moritz writes poetry plays and poems. Over thirty plays have received professional production. Venues include: **Public Theater**, **BACA Downtwon**, **Freedom Theater**, **Theatre Double**, **Painted Bride**, **Here**, **Nuyorican**, **St. Marks**, **Bowery Poetry Club**, **Stickies**. His work appears in the *Nuyorican Theatre Anthology*. **United Artists Books**, the long time poetry press, will publish his second collection of plays in 2017.

David Moscovich //

David Moscovich is the Romanian-American author of *You Are Make Very Important Bathtime* (JEF Books, Chicago, IL) and *LIFE+70 [Redacted]*, a print version of the single most expensive literary e-book ever to be hacked (Lit Fest Press.) He edits **Louffa Press**, a micro-press dedicated to printing innovative fiction and artist books. He lives in New York City.

KB Nemcosky //

KB Nemcosky was a reading coordinator at **Chez LaRoe**, 1997-2001. He is the author of two books: *Drift* (Ten Pell Books, 2000) and *dear friend* (Straw Gate Books, 2012). His work has appeared in *Tamarind*, *The Unbearables Collection*, *Pagan Place*, *Chez Chez*, *Gathering of the Tribes*, *Press 1*, *Push New York*, among others. KB Nemcosky lives in New York City.

Valery Oisteanu //

Valery Oisteanu is a poet, writer, and artist of the avant-garde. Born in USSR (1943) and educated in Romania. He debuted with *PROSTHESIS* in 1970 (Litera Press, Bucharest). At the age of 20, he adopted Dada and Surrealism as a philosophy of art and life and a few years later, English as his primary language. Immigrating to New York City in 1972, he has been writing in English for the past 44 years. He is the author of 13 books of poetry, a book of short fiction, *The King of Penguins* (Linear Art Press, 2000) and a book of essays (in progress), *The AVANT-GODS*. A new book of VisPo (Visual Poetry) collages titled *Lighter than Air* in Spuyten Duyvil Press NYC (2017).

Jennifer-Leigh Oprihory //

Jennifer-Leigh Oprihory is a connoisseur of carpe diem and light. A NJ-born, Washington, D.C.-based multimedia investigative journalist, editor, and page and performance poet, she holds an M.S. in Journalism from Northwestern University's Medill School of Journalism, Media, Integrated Marketing Communications, and a B.A. in English Literature and Writing from New Jersey City University. Follow her on Twitter & Instagram @ jenniferleigho.

Yuko Otomo //

Yuko Otomo. Japanese origin. A bilingual (Japanese & English) poet & a visual artist. She also writes haiku, art criticism & essays. She has read in St. Mark's Poetry Project, Tribes, Bowery Poetry Club, ABC No Rio, La Mama, The Living Theatre, PS1, MoMA, The Queens Museum, etc & in Japan, France & Germany. Her publication includes "Garden: Selected Haiku" (**Beehive Press**), "A Sunday Afternoon on the Isle of Museum" (**Propaganda Press**), "PINK" (**Sisyphus Press**), "Small Poems" (**Ugly Duckling Presse**), "The Hand of The Poet" (**UDP**), "STUDY & Other Poems on Art" (**UDP**) & "Elements" (**the Feral Press**). She exhibited her artwork at Court House Gallery @ Anthology Film Archives, Tribes Gallery & Vision Festival, etc. She is a contributing writer for a collective art critical forum www.Arteidolia.com currently. Yuko is a 2015 Pushcart Prize nominee.

Mireya Perez //

Mireya Perez's poetry searches for that "other voice" breaking through entrapment and oppression, the fragile markers to unearth more hidden voices. Her work appears in *Revista del Hada*, *Caribbean Review*, *Americas Review*, *Diosas en Bronce: Anthology of Colombian Women Writers*, *IRP Voices*, among others.

Puma Perl //

Puma Perl is a performer, producer and published writer/poet. She's the author of two chapbooks, *Belinda and Her Friends*, and *Ruby True*, and two full-length collections, *knuckle tattoos*, and *Retrograde*. She performs spoken word with her band, **Puma Perl and Friends**, and is the creator/curator of the **Pandemonium**, which merges poetry and rock and roll. She was the recipient of a **New York City Press Award** for her journalistic work, and of the 2016 **Acker Award** in writing.

A. Podracky //

A. Podracky lives in Queens, New York. Her work has appeared in a variety of journals, including *Hanging Loose*, *WSQ*, *Newtown Literary*, the *Montauk Anthology*, *Siblings: A Wising Up Anthology*.

Ron Price //

Ron Price teaches at the Juilliard School. His most recent collection is *A True Account Of The Failure Of Bodies To Adequately Burn*.

J D Rage //

J D Rage writes poetry and novels, paints and takes photographs and often appears in strange places for no good reason. J D publishes *CURARE* magazine and runs **Venom Press**.

Jill Rapaport //

Jill Rapaport's collection of fiction, *Duchamp et Moi and Other Stories*, was published by Fly by Night Press / A Gathering of the Tribes in 2014.

Thaddeus Rutkowski //

Thaddeus Rutkowski is the author of the books *Violent Outbursts, Haywire, Tetched,* and *Roughhouse. Haywire* won the **Members Choice Award**, given by the **Asian American Writers Workshop**. He teaches at Medgar Evers College and the Writer's Voice of the West Side YMCA. He received a fiction writing fellowship from the **New York Foundation for the Arts**.

Sarah Sarai //

"A poet of sensitivity, Sarah Sarai filters through the vast junk of daily life." - Krystal Languell in *Pleiades Journal.* Sarai was born in New York State and lives in New York City. Find her on Facebook, at **My 3000 Loving Arms** (blogspot), or on a barstool. The poem "Love Letter" is From *Geographies of Soul and Taffeta*, Indolent Books, 2016.

Ilka Scobie //

Ilka Scobie is a native New Yorker. Her recent poems appear in *Glitter Mob, Urban Graffiti* and here / there. She is a deputy editor of *Live Mag.* She writes about contemporary art for *London ArtLyst* and *White Hot.* She co-curated a group show Art Am 3 in Soncino, Italy with her husband, Luigi Cazzaniga.

Hugh Seidman //

Hugh Seidman has published six books. His last, *Somebody Stand Up And Sing*, won the **Green Rose Prize** from **New Issues Press**. His first, *Collecting Evidence*, won the **Yale Younger Poets Prize**. He has received multiple NY State and NEA poetry grants and has taught writing at Wisconsin, Yale, William and Mary, the New School, and other institutions. Acknowledgements: 1. *Crossing Bryant Park: The Café Review and High Chair* (**www.highchair.com.ph**). *For Jayne: The Laurel Review.*

Brian Sheffield //

Brian Sheffield is a poet from California living in Brooklyn and is pretty sure that he takes himself way too seriously. He is immature and talks about himself way too much. He has taught in various public school and university classrooms and has been published a few anthologies, journals, and zines. Oh yeah, he also has chapbooks.

Susan Sherman //

Susan Sherman: Most recent books are *Nirvana on Ninth Street*, short Fiction with photos by Colleen McKay and *An Afterward by Rona L. Holub* (Wings Press, Fall, 2014); *The Light that Puts an End to Dreams: New and Selected Poems* (Wings Press, 2012); *America's Child: A Woman's Journey through the Radical Sixties*, a memoir (Curbstone / Northwestern University Press, 2007). She has survived living and writing in the East Village / Lower East Side for over fifty years.

John Silver //

John Silver grew up Cold Spring Harbor, L.I. Did covers, poems for *Tamarind*. Hosted **Tamarind Collation** for 10 years. Moved to Westbeth, Published in *And Then*, and other anthologies. Hosted Westbeth readings. Curator of *The Image and The Word Exhibition* at the Westbeth Gallery. 2 Books (Underfield Press). Contributed covers and poems to *White Rabbit*.

Miriam Stanley //

Miriam Stanley is published in several anthologies including *Grabbing the Apple*, *Occupy Wall Street*, and *Skyscrapers, Taxis, and Tampons*. She also has three books of poems published by Rogue Scholars Press: *Let's Fly To Trazodone*, *Get Over It!*, and *Not To Be Believed*. Miriam Stanley has performed in Israel and the United States.

Terese Svoboda //

Terese Svoboda's *When The Next Big War Blows Down The Valley: Selected and New Poems* (Anhinga) was published last year, and *Professor Harriman's Steam Air-Ship* (Eyewear), her seventh book of poetry, this year.

Lawrence Swan //

Lawrence Swan is a painter and poet who has lived in Brooklyn since 1998. He was born in Lexington, Kentucky in 1954 and grew up in Palm Beach County. He received his BFA in painting at the Cleveland Institute of Art in 1981 and earned an MA in philosophy at Cleveland State University in 1986. The idea is to make poetry with whatever spirit or matter is at hand.

Alice B. Talkless //

Alice B. Talkless is Ronna Lebo, a poet, musician and painter who has performed in the NY scene for over twenty years. She is co-founder of Black Square Editions, a non-profit press for poetry and art. She is also co-founder of Reservoir Art Space in Ridgewood, Queens, which includes private studios and an experimental gallery for visual arts.

J M Theisen de González **//**

J M received her 1st rejection letter at 9 from *Readers Digest* (Gramps submitted an essay about Lucky the hamster). Previous: "E Village Eye", "Waterfront Week" (columnist), "The Curse", "Pink Pages", "Juice", "Curare", Right Bank Charleston, Knitting Factory, Nuyorican, & McManus Cafes, Pussycat Lounge. Spain: La Llotja Hotel, Colón, Bar Babia. Also: NYCACC volunteer.

Jack Thomas **//**

Following a (major) retrospective @ PRINTED MATTER (this past spring), Jack Thomas is calculating his next move (taking it on the road: Canada, San Francisco, Mexico). Why I Persist!, an introduction to the memoir, AVAILABLE @ A WALL NEAR YOU!, which was read @ The Annual New Year's Day Reading (@ Nuyorican) 2(-)years ago, appears (in print) for the first time (anywhere)!

Zev Torres **//**

Zev Torres' poetry has appeared in numerous print and on-line publications including, *Literary Orphans*, **Five2One**'s online publication *#thesideshow*, the *Suisun Valley Review* and *Xanadu*. In 2010, Zev founded the **Skewered Syntax Poetry Crawls** and, since 2008, has hosted **Make Music New York**'s annual **Spoken Word Spectacular**.

Anoek Van Praag //

Born in The Netherlands, Anoek van Praag earned degrees in Trauma Counseling and a Teachers degree in The Performing Arts. Presently she teaches at The College for Health Sciences, works at Equinox and has a private practice. Anoek began writing Poetry at a very early age. She writes and reads in Dutch, English, French and Italian. Her poems are published in various books and magazines such as *Maintenant 7, 8 and 9* (Three Rooms Press), *Marymark Broadsheets Series*, *Nomadic Choir* and can be found on YouTube and on-line magazines. She is performing monthly at **Monologues and Madnessher** at Cornelia Street café.

Claire Van Winkle //

Claire Van Winkle is a poet, essayist, and literary translator. She currently teaches creative writing, composition, literature, and grammar at Queens College, Queensborough Community College, and the Fashion Institute of Technology. In addition to her creative and academic pursuits, Claire works as a Recreational Therapist (RT) at the New York State Psychiatric Institute. Her clinical work and research focus on the development and implementation of Pedagogical Therapy, which applies linguistic theory and creative writing workshop methods to one-on-one and group therapy sessions for inpatient psychiatric patients.

Phyllis Wat //

Phyllis Wat's books are *Shadow Blue*, *The Fish Soup Bowl Expedition*, and from United Artists Books, *The Influence of Painings Hung in Bedrooms*, as well as *Wu Going There*.

Bruce Weber **//**
_____

Bruce Weber is the founder and organizer of **The Alternative New Year's Day Spoken Word / Performance Extravaganza** (ANYDSWPE). He is the author of five books of poetry, including *The Breakup of My First Marriage* (Rogue Scholars Press). By day, Bruce is Curator of **Paintings & Sculpture** at the **Museum of the City of New York**.

Francine Witte **//**
_____

Francine Witte is a poet, flash fiction writer, photographer, blogger, and reviewer. Her latest chapbook, *Not All Fires Burn the Same* won the **2016 Slipstream Chapbook Competition** and was recently published by them. She is a former high school English teacher. She lives in NYC. "Selfie at the End of the World" was originally published in *Crab Creek Review*. "My Dead Florida Mother Meets Gandhi" was originally published in *Slippery Elm*.

Jeffrey Cyphers Wright **//**
_____

Jeffrey Cyphers Wright is a poet, artist, critic, eco-activist, and impresario. He also edits and publishes *Live Mag!* His 13th book is a manifesto titled *Party Everywhere*. Wright's poem "Staggering Love" originally appeared in New Verse News.

Anton Yakovlev **//**
_____

Born in Moscow, Russia, Anton Yakovlev studied filmmaking and poetry at Harvard University. He is the author of chapbooks *Ordinary Impalers* (2017), *The Ghost of Grant Wood* (2015), and *Neptune Court* (2015). His poems have appeared in *The New Yorker*, The *Hopkins Review*, *Prelude*, and elsewhere. His book of translations of poetry by Sergei Esenin is forthcoming in 2017.

ALPHABETICAL INDEX OF POEMS

•

ROGUE SCHOLARS
Press

For General Information, go to:

http://www.roguescholars.com

For more information or a price quote for our
book design and editing services, contact:

editor@roguescholars.com

•

Other ANYDSWPE Volumes:

Palabras Luminosas (Luminous Words) - 2016
Rogue Scholars Press
ISBN-13: 978-0-9840982-3-1

Shadow Of The Geode (Sombra Del Geode) - 2015
Bonsai Publishers
ISBN-13: 978-1-9424630-0-9 (1st Edition)

Estrellas En El Fuego (Stars In The Fire) - 2014
Rogue Scholars Press
ISBN-13: 978-0-9840982-9-3

•

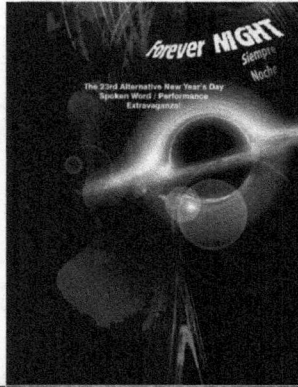

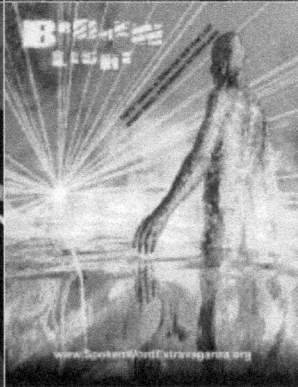